# Collecting Figural Doorstops

# Collecting Figural Doorstops

*Marilyn G. Hamburger*
*Beverly S. Lloyd*

Photography by Jay Hoffman

South Brunswick and New York: A. S. Barnes and Company
London: Thomas Yoseloff Ltd

© 1978 by A. S. Barnes and Co., Inc.

A. S. Barnes and Co., Inc.
Cranbury, New Jersey 08512

Thomas Yoseloff Ltd
Magdalen House
136-148 Tooley Street
London SE1 2TT, England

**Library of Congress Cataloging in Publication Data**

Hamburger, Marilyn G    1941-
   Collecting figural doorstops.

   Bibliography: p.
   Includes index.
   1. Doorstops—Collectors and collecting. I. Lloyd,
Beverly S., 1934-    joint author.    II.    Title.
NK4894.6.H35        745.1        76-50219
ISBN 0-498-02082-7

PRINTED IN THE UNITED STATES OF AMERICA

# Contents

Preface 7

Acknowledgments 9

1 Development of the Figural Doorstop 13

2 A Short History of Iron Manufacture 43

3 Patents, Trademarks, and Reproductions 54

Appendix 67

Bibliography 97

Index 99

# Preface

This is a book about doorstops. For more than twenty centuries man has been busy casting metal objects. The progress of these objects depended not only on the technology of the time but also on the events of the era. This was particularly true in England and no less so in the United States, where great and small foundries contributed their artistic doorstop creations to the production of this vital cultural and folk-art area. Figural doorstops have been much overlooked because they were a stepchild to the more impressive machinery and other gaudy equipment produced by the giant furnaces; however, doorstops have remained, while many of the larger trappings have rusted away. It may not be for the original utilitarian purpose but for their intrinsic beauty that we cherish these floor antiques.

This book has been compiled to meet the wants of those who own old doorstops and would like to know more about them, and to stimulate others to whom the fascination of doorstop collecting is as yet unknown.

Doorstops appeal to those who are part historian, utilizing doorstops as a barometer of past events, and to those who are part sentimentalist.

Doorstop collecting appeals to people in many walks of life, especially those who wish to rejoice in the cultivation of an interest that provides agreeable food for reflection, stimulation, and relaxation—all this and more may be found within the limits of a collection of antique doorstops.

# Acknowledgments

We would like to thank those who have given us help and information concerning the writing of this book. We are especially indebted to Abraham Hirsch for his valuable suggestions and information; to Victoria D. Hirsch for her advice on the illustrations; and to Jay Hoffman for his magnificent job of photographing the doorstops.

Our most grateful thanks, however, go to the foundrymen whose memories of doorstop production and their willingness to share these past experiences have greatly enriched our knowledge. They include Hunter Earhart, Superintendent, Virginia Metalcrafters, Waynesboro, Virginia; Evans Foundry, St. Michaels, Maryland; Mrs. Friend, Hubley Manufacturing Company, Lancaster, Pennsylvania; Dudley G. Gould, Technical Publications, Editor, American Foundrymen's Society; Mr. Jessie Pond, McLean, Virginia; Edward B. Watkins, St. Michaels, Maryland; and Mr. Whyte, Brunnerville, Pennsylvania.

We greatly appreciate the courtesy extended to us by the museums, libraries, Patent Office in Washington, D.C., and others who cooperated in providing information necessary to our research.

Additional thanks to W.E. Long and K. Halstead, who kindly put their private collections at the writers' disposal.

Above all, we wish to express our gratitude to our husbands for their encouragement and help in the many phases of planning and work that have resulted in this book.

# Collecting Figural Doorstops

# 1
# Development of The Figural Doorstop

*Doorstops As Collectibles*

Doorstops are unique. They are representative of a vital folk-art development. Although doorstops have assumed a humble place in the palace of antiques, they represent an effort to take them a step away from stark practicality to the creation of beauty. Criteria of beauty differ with development of culture and the human comprehension of art—therein lies the fundamental purpose for studying the cast-iron figural doorstop.

Part of the difficulty in appreciating the charm of these creations is that many are collectibles but not pure antiques. True, they were produced well into the 1930s and even the early 1940s, but with a little investigation one will find that the first doorstops date to the last quarter of the eighteenth century; therefore, if the modern-day definition of an antique contains any validity, then figural doorstops must be included.

Certainly, few would agree that a doorstop is a prime antique, although there exist certain ones—especially early English brass and bronze doorporters—that meet the criteria of a fine antique. However, there is no argument that figural doorstops are a prime collectible.

One rationale for collecting them may be that American doorstops meet the requirements of folk art. The form was designed from familiar models. The accomplishment of the finished product demanded skill but no rigorous schooling. The accent of color or fanciful form added gaiety to the home. The piece was easily identifiable.

Another remaining criterion is that no new forms are being executed. Iron foundries are decreasing in number and, of those remaining, only a few are manufacturing the figural doorstop. Seemingly, these works are simply copies of the older yesteryear subjects; therefore, the number of original doorstops with their intriguing shapes and fanciful colors are diminishing from the American scene.

The sophisticated collector of today will be hard put to come upon an early doorstop in mint condition. Still, for the connoisseur, a wide range of subject matter remains. One may choose animals, celebrities, ships, baskets of flowers, or a host of varied themes. A collection of only one period would be interesting—one might elect Victorian or perhaps Art Deco.

*Earliest Known Doorporters*

Prior to the advent of electric fans and air conditioners a doorstop was required to enable a door to remain open so cool, fresh air might enter the interior of a room. A large stone was probably utilized as the first doorstop, or, as the English say, doorporter. But man, not content with anything so ordinary, took a step toward decorative beauty and combined it with function. At the instant the idea was executed, the first figural doorporter sprang into existence. The data concerning the exact origin of this figural doorporter is fragmentary; however, a mechanism was invented in 1775 by two Englishmen named John Izon and Thomas Whitehurst—these two are credited with developing a cast brass "rising hinge with steel roller" that enabled a door to elevate slightly when opened so that it would slowly ease itself shut. This innovation was a boon, especially for homes with slanting wooden floors and sagging hinges that forced the door to close without provocation.

Among the earliest type of doorporter was a full-form solid iron or brass

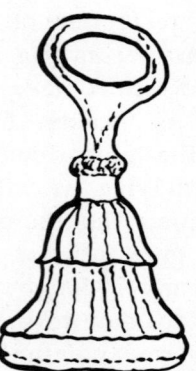

1. *Early nineteenth-century cast-iron, English short-handled, half-bell doorporter.*

2. *Regency pineapple doorporter. In reproduction form.*

*3. Brass horse on plinth—typical early English doorporter.*

piece with a long thin shaft rising from the center of the weight. This shaft was topped by a plain loop handle. A more elaborate doorporter design in this style resembled a polished brass flower basket, cast in the round, with a long rod rising from the center into a solid finial handle. Instead of a loop, the finial was a realistically formed pineapple—a most striking example of early English workmanship.

During the 1790s a flat-backed doorporter was introduced that stood firmly against the door. This style consisted of a base shaped like half a bell, with a long rod topped by a plain ring. The earliest doorporters had long thin handles; however, by the beginning of the nineteenth century, many weights were being produced without them. In the 1820s, handle patterns became more elaborate, often appearing in the shape of a pineapple, the symbol of hospitality. Others sported a ball rather than the earlier ring form. Some of the iron ones may have had a bronze finish and brass handles. The doorporter of this period often rested on a base called a "plinth."

By the late Regency period, such cumbersome pieces as crouching sphinxes, winged leopards, seated lions, and a peacock on a fence were introduced. Most of these designs had no handles. The modification of the earlier half-bell design emerged, consisting of a lion's paw or a ball beneath the half-bell. This Regency design was comprised of a lion's paw, in iron or brass, with a band above the paw and a stylized acanthus leaf on the rod, ending in a twisted ropelike handle. The weight of doorporters in this period

*4. Reproduction of English Regency peacock on a fence—American replica.*

could have been up to twelve pounds; some stood as high as eighteen inches. Regardless, the fascination of these pieces is unquestionable.

One early producer of the solitary paw type of porter was Kenrick, Smith and Company of 24 Legge Street, Birmingham, England. They embossed their weights with the trademark *KENRICK* in capital letters. This mark is located on the back of the piece.

*5. Regency brass lion's-paw doorporter: an adaptation of the half-bell design. (In reproduction.)*

6. *Charming Staffordshire cottage doorporter. Late nineteenth century.*

*Stoneware*

As time progressed, doorporters became a more creative form of folk sculpture. The most popular materials used for early doorporters were brass, iron, glass, and stoneware. A charming category of collectibles is the stoneware cottages and castles.

A choice doorporter not readily known to the collector is the large, heavy stoneware cottages made from the early years of the nineteenth century. Not only Rockingham pottery but many other well-known factories and individual potteries, largely in Staffordshire towns, produced weights of this type. A popular doorporter during the 1840s was one copied from Copeland's model of Shakespeare's house at Stratford-on-Avon. This piece is in white stoneware with painted roof and beams. Apart from Old World cottages, there were turreted castle gateways, churches, circular tollhouses, summerhouses, farm buildings, and flowery garden arbors.

These quaint cottages were often enhanced by the use of floral encrustation on the roof, walls, and base. Texture was given by using shavings of paste scattered on the glaze before firing. The late nineteenth-century Staffordshire cottage pictured has a white ground, with Gothic-style windows and front stairs outlined in gold. Flowers and vines lazily ramble across the front of the cottage. Shades of pink and apple green are used as accents.

Some of the best stoneware doorporters came from Rockingham, Coalport, Worcester, and Derby between 1820-1860. Copies of these cottages have been made and often were properly aged at the necessary pressure points. The newer pieces are usually handsome and nicely modeled, but they lack the detail and distinction of the early nineteenth-century originals.

In America, a Rockingham glaze earthenware doorstop, in the form of a dog, was produced in Ohio about 1850. These dogs were made in redware, yellow-ware, and brownware. They are now part of the collection at the Brooklyn Museum in New York.

*Glass*

Since doorporters come in unique shapes and materials they are often not recognized as a stop by the dealer or collector. Many large glass doorporters, or "dumps" as they are called by the West Country of England, are mistakenly thought to be oversized paperweights.

A typical dump ranges from three to six inches high, is shaped like a beehive, and can weigh up to six pounds. These unsophisticated pieces usually encased air-bubbles, vague floral forms, or a combination of both within a clear green glass.

The necessary ingredients to make a dump were several simple tools and clear green glass, commonly used for bottles during the nineteenth century. The gatherer took a hollow tube called a "blowpipe," inserted the heated end into the pot of glass, and twirled it until it contained a molten mass the shape of an egg. Chalk was then scattered in a desired pattern on a flat slab called a "marver." Soft glass was pressed upon the chalk, then more hot glass was quickly added to cover the whole. The hot glass hitting the chalk caused gas to form, which was encased within the dome, creating a thin film of tiny, glistening bubbles. The resulting effects of this method included abstract cascading waterfalls, a plant growing in a pot, or an airy floral motif.

To obtain bubbles of entrapped air within the dome, molten glass was

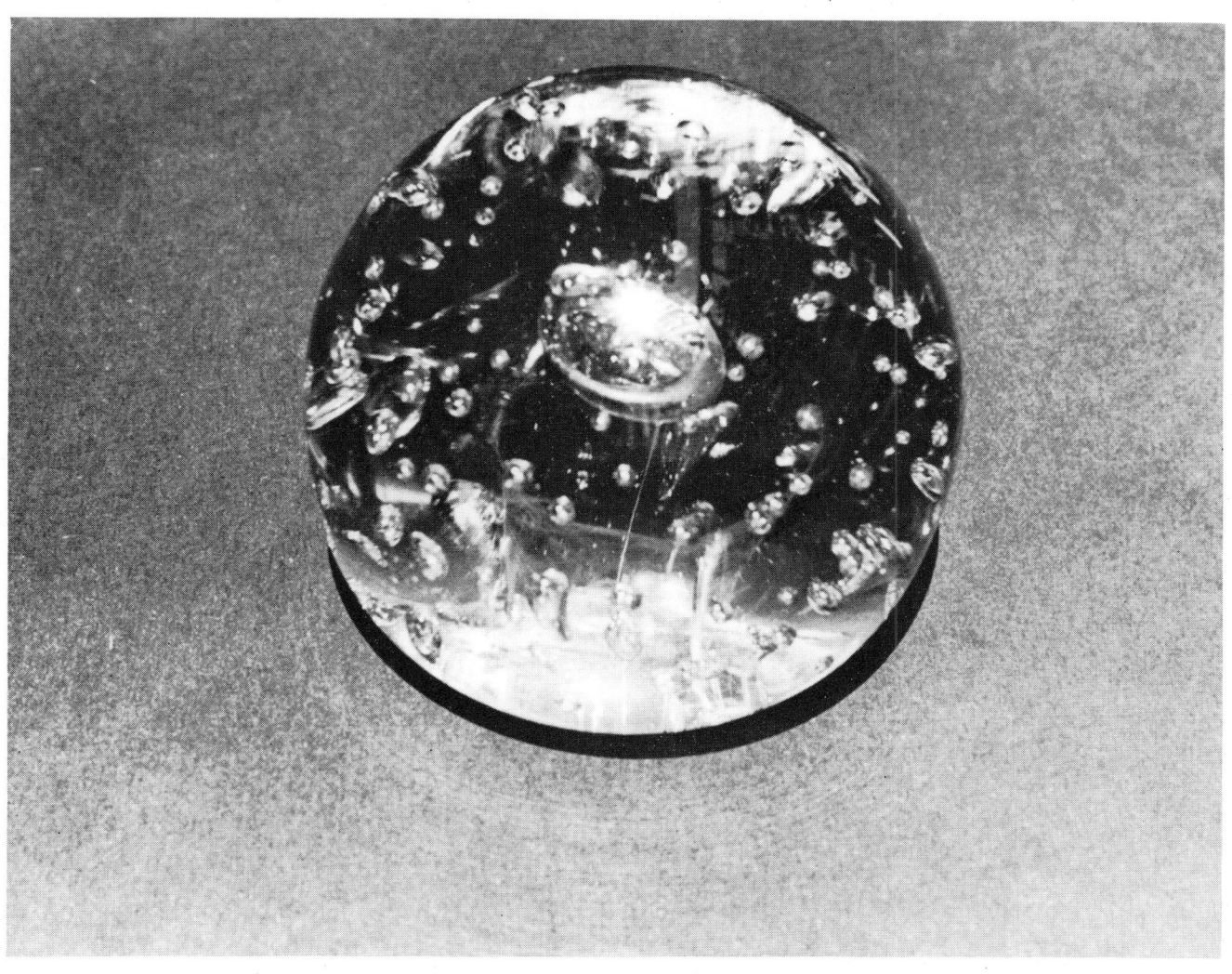

*7. Classic glass dump with entrapped air bubbles.*

dented with holes by a sharp tool; then more hot glass was smoothly applied over the resulting air pockets.

On occasion, pear-shaped bubbles with a silvery filament at the narrowed end may be found. This motif is created by quickly piercing the soft glass with a cold sharp instrument, which has a thin wire attached. The tool is then sharply withdrawn and the second gather is applied over the depression, producing a pyriform bubble that tapers to a mere wisp of hair. Several of these bubbles captured in glass create the illusion of balloons floating in air.

On cruder dumps the center of the base was left concave, showing the fracture point where the piece was separated from the pontil rod. To flatten the base of free-blown doorporters, they were simply pressed down on any flat surface. The rough marks from the pontil rod were ground or polished off the finer glass specimens but continued to remain on the low-cost production items. Most local glasshouses in the north of England made dumps; also, traveling glass blowers made and "hawked" them. Quite often, the dump was custom ordered by the purchaser, then handcrafted by men who were experts through years of experience in blowing glassware.

Both Bristol and Nailsea produced glass doorporters from 1828 on. Several years later, dumps were also being blown at Birmingham, Castleford, and Stourbridge. A few weights have been located that are stamped J. Kilner, Wakefield—but these are rare.

Green glass weights were generally made by glasshouses that produced handmade bottles; thus, when automation superseded hand processes, their manufacture ceased. Research shows that dumps were made through the first third of the twentieth century, but it is almost impossible to distinguish the early specimens from later pieces.

Clear flint glass was used for porters from the 1840s on. Because of the weight of the lead oxide, the flint glass appears to have a smoky cast. Motifs such as cascading bubbles, flowers in a pot, and flowers of green, blue, purple, red, and yellow with tiny bubbles on the petals were popular items. An unusual doorporter was shown at the 1887 Jubilee that encased a ceramic bust of Queen Victoria. It was produced by a glassworks at Knottingley and is now part of the Tolson Memorial Museum, Huddersfield, England.

The milliflori style was popular during the 1850s in both paperweights and doorporters. These beauties of skillfully devised circles, spirals, wheels, and florets of brilliant color appear to be suspended by magic within the shining crystal dome. Much of the charm of these dumps is lost if exclusively appreciated as oversized paperweights. Lucky the collector who discovers among his treasures a dump, for the real beauty of these specimens is most enjoyed when viewed as a floor antique and not as just another paperweight.

*Early Wooden Specimens*

Late eighteenth- and nineteenth-century wooden doorporters would be a rare find for any serious collector. A ready supply of wood allowed this type of folk art to flourish. The most candid glimpses of a nation's heritage are seen in amateur wood carvings done for a specific purpose and not solely for the sake of art. The beauty of the carving is that each piece is unique and, unlike metal sculpture, cannot be duplicated in a mold.

*8. Late eighteenth-century English wood, folk-art doorporter.*

Research has shown two wooden examples of charming primitive pieces. One, a whimsical English variety of the late eighteenth century, was carved into the shape of a pig greedily eating from a slop bowl. The pig was then painted for greater realism. The other is a black and white, full-formed primitive-cat doorstop. This piece dates from the second half of the nineteenth century, was carved by a Pennsylvania craftsman, and is housed in the Newark Museum, Newark, New Jersey.

*Marble*

Marble has always been a favorite material of sculptors because of its beauty and the ease with which it is worked. It therefore seems natural that a reasonable amount of doorstops should have been produced in this medium. The shape that appears most often is a rectangular block similar in appearance to a brick.

Two variations of the bricklike shape are pictured. One is a solid piece of white marble with graceful, arched legs. The entire stop has been carved from a single block. The second brick is made of two different pieces of marble—one pink, the other grey. The upper section of the brick is fastened to the lower part by a bolt—this bolt also anchors the cast-iron loop handle

*9. Solid marble with graceful, arched legs.*

to the marble. Note the different type of leg. It is short, stubby, and carved from the lower section of marble.

Still another example, this one without legs or handle, belongs to a family on the Eastern Shore of Maryland. The brick was commissioned by a member of the family. This nineteenth-century piece bears the surname *WATKINS* on the surface.

*10. Underside of arched leg marble doorstop.*

Decorative patterns were sometimes carved on marble doorstops. One such piece has a rose design, with petals and leaves radiating symmetrically from the center. A similar brick belongs to the Smithsonian Institution, Washington, D. C., but instead of a rose it is embellished with a pear.

The United States has large supplies of marble. The two leading quarries are in Tennessee and Vermont. English Derbyshire marble in the shape of bricks and obelisks was also popular during the mid-nineteenth century. Unless a marble "stop" bears an inscription or signature, giving one a clue to its origin, it would be difficult to identify which country produced the doorstop.

11. *Two-piece marble brick with cast-iron loop handle.*

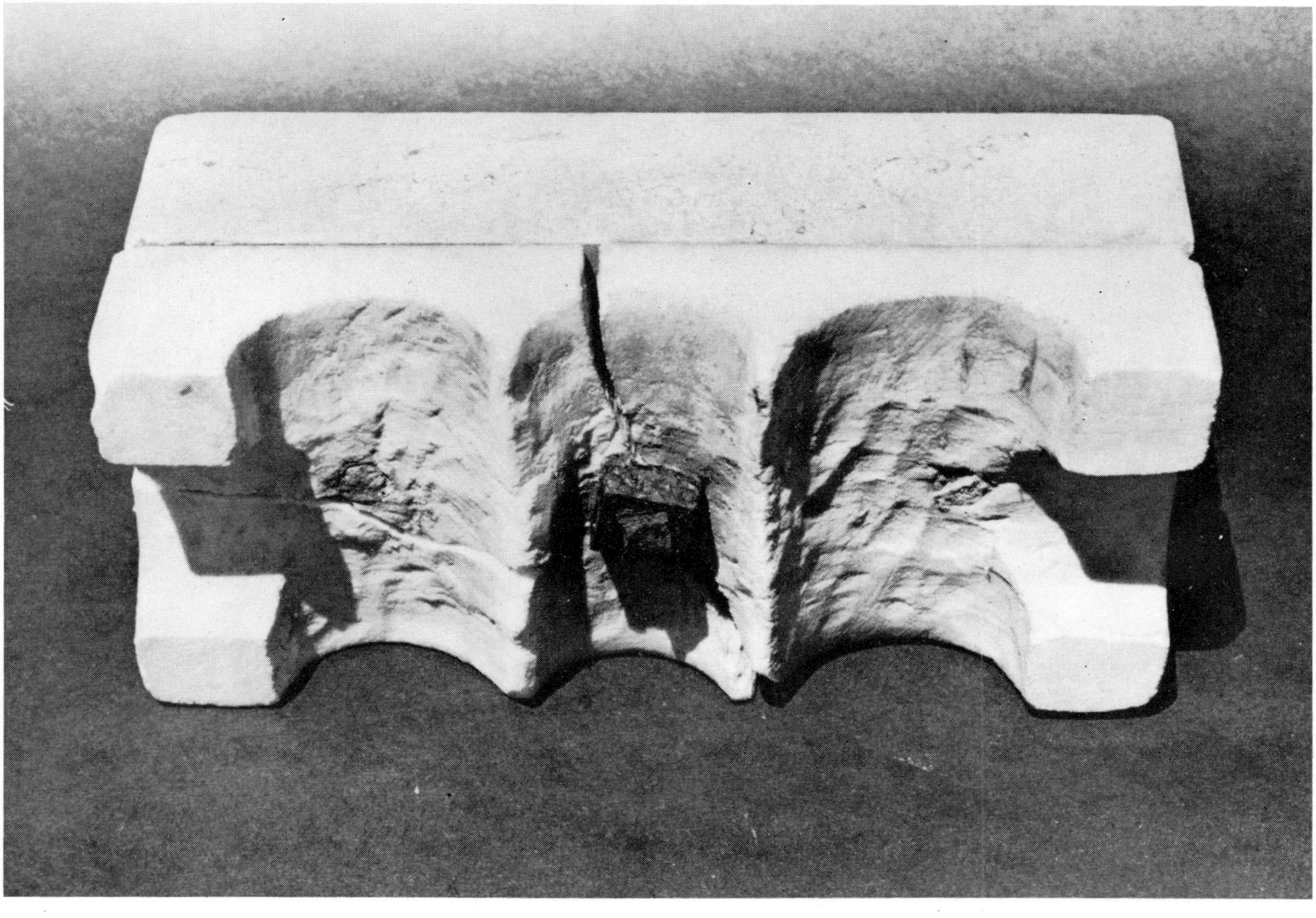

## Victoriana

While there are specialized doorstops that are housed in museums, they are not likely to be encountered in today's market. There are, however, scores of unique doorstops to be found, and they are made of diverse materials and subject matter. There is excellent potential for those who seek only one category of doorstops. One may choose fruit or flower baskets, commemorative figures or Aesop's fables, animals or mythical figures. Some humorous and some naughty were produced. Doorstops emerged in the shape of lions, dwarfs, hunters, horses, cupids, swans, griffins, historical buildings, and countless other fantastic creations of elaborate character.

In the 1820s the overflowing cornucopia was a popular English subject. By 1830, brass regimental porters were highly esteemed and included those that incorporated the coat-of-arms of the original owner. During this early period, full-length celebrity figures with a bronzed, cast-iron finish were in vogue. These doorporters were designed in the likeness of a famous person or to commemorate an important event; thus, over the years, a parade of sturdy flat-backed figures, often designed to be lifted easily, were produced for the public.

Such notables as Wellington with a cocked hat, Punch with a curved cap, and an odd assortment of British monarchs have been portrayed as doorporters.

By now the Victorians believed that the bigger and more lavishly decorated metal works were the best. The Coalbrookdale Company

*13. Pornographic frog with nude lady on reverse side. Circa 1830.*

14. *Elaborate English Regency swan doorporter. Neck is used as a handle. (In reproduction.)*

15. *Majestic cast-iron lion doorporter produced by St. Blazey Foundry— England, circa 1850.*

16. *Soldier doorporter on plinth, with cocked hat and sword. Circa 1840.*

*17. English doorporter representing Stevenson's early train named "Locomotion." Circa 1825.*

displayed its metal work, iron and bronze, at the Crystal Palace Exhibition of 1851. Many of their pieces were widely acclaimed by the critics of that day. This iron-founding company was in the forefront of the Victorian craze for decorative ironwork.

An impressive highlight of this exhibition was the elegant bronze doorporters created by Mr. Andy Handyside, Britannia Foundry of Derby. An unusual display by Messrs. Simcox and Pemperton, of Birmingham, dealt with many fine specimens of useful fittings for the home. Such pieces as curtain bands, bell pulls, door handles, and curtain ornaments were displayed. These types of pieces were largely ignored by the artistic designer until 1851. It is probable that this company also produced doorporters as part of their home-decoration line.

Eventually, the Coalbrookdale Company came to monopolize the sale of fine-quality doorporters because of its reputation for artistic design and finely burnished pieces. Some examples of Coalbrookdale's doorporters are whippets, deer, and eagles. A more interesting specimen is a seventeen-inch bronzed armoured knight with a spear and shield under a medieval canopy. This piece may carry an inscription on the back of the plinth: THE COALBROOKDALE COMPANY, REGISTERED, OCTOBER 28TH, 1841. There are modern reproductions of the knight, but these are slightly smaller due to the metal-casting process.

It isn't surprising that the popular personality idea represented by Punch became a vehicle for other creations, out of which British ironmongers developed an extensive line of doorporters. Punch and his dog of painted iron or in brass appear in the second quarter of the nineteenth century. This figure was based on the "Punch" of the famous satirical magazine series that

*18. Gothic knight. Circa 1841. (In reproduction.)*

first appeared in June 1841. His companion, "Judy," or "Judy with Baby," also appeared in cast-iron or brass. In a more humorous vein the small, ill-clad Ally Sloper appeared a quarter of a century later. He was based on the character that evolved from the magazine *Judy* early in the 1870s.

*19. A satirical Punch doorporter based on character from 1841 magazine.*

By the 1820s in America, the domestic production of iron articles was catching up to the needs of this infant nation. During this period, cast-iron buildings were favored. Architects designed the facades to resemble Italian palazzi, which were usually built of marble and stucco worked in a very extravagant manner. Iron, of course, may be cast to look like anything, and since marble was costly and often inappropriate, iron did very nicely once it was painted in stonelike colors.

In 1824, Andrew Jackson was one of five candidates for the United States

*20. A handsome English couple—an original Punch and rare Judy sporting bright paint. Last half of the nineteenth century.*

presidency. In 1828, he became the seventh president of the United States. His campaign was skillfully managed by his friend and advisor, William B. Lewis. Among the many campaign gimmicks used to ensure success was a cast-iron frog doorstop bearing the slogan: "I croak for the Jackson Wagon."

Although American cast-iron doorstops were manufactured from the first decade of the nineteenth century, it was not until after the Civil War that the metal was used extensively.

The cast-iron passion that enveloped the United States during the 1860s and 1870s has often been referred to as "ferromania." This was the time when America's desire for anything iron and its advancing technology teamed with artistic endeavors to produce many sorts of interesting metal objects. Showing off cast-iron elegancies for the home and lawn was a distinctive sign of upper-class affluence.

From this iron craze came the desire for fanciful American doorstops.

Brunnerville Foundry in Brunnerville, Pennsylvania, was a small jobbing plant from 1850 until the late 1960s. Flower-basket doorstops were cast and painted in this geographic area from 1875 until the foundry closed. The products of this small plant are often pictured in antique publications. A prime example of high Victorian metal art is a basket of flowers manufactured at Brunnerville.

Apart from the influence of the English doorporter design on American examples, mention should also be made of the strong influence of the German communities of Pennsylvania. Their folk designs include such favorite motifs as the tulip, rose, iris, and other floral forms. One may encounter iron doorstops with doves, distelfinks, and hearts interwoven into the main theme of the weight. Also utilized are heraldic designs and such medieval symbols as the cock, stag, fish, and double-headed eagle.

The 1876 Centennial that was held for a six-month period in Philadelphia's Fairmount Park was an international exhibition of manufactured arts, agriculture, and mineral products. This exposition was not merely a fair but was the official observance of the first one-hundred years of American independence.

*21. Brunnerville Foundry where many American doorstops were produced.*

22. *Regional Victorian flower basket from Brunnerville.*

23. *Lovely rendition of Pennsylvania German folk-art basket of tulips. Circa 1870.*

   The Centennial celebration spawned a tremendous assortment of objects to commemorate this historic event. Among the most interesting items were glassware, china, medals, doorstops, banks, and paperweights.
   A cast-iron doorstop in the image of George Washington was likely cast in tribute to this great patriot. The rigid pose and facial features are accented by paint. The colorful old paint is worn, but this only enhances the folk-art detail.
   An enchanting figural doorstop reminiscent of Jenny Lind was produced during the last quarter of the nineteenth century. The "Swedish Nightingale" had successfully toured the United States between 1850 and 1852. The doorstop portrayal stands nine inches tall and is painted in cream and other naturalistic colors. The model sustains a frozen curtsey position similar to one she may have used while accepting the adulation of the audience at the end of one of her florid cadenzas.

24. *An admirable folk-art rendition of George Washington.*

*Lovely rendition of Pennsylvania German folk art basket of tulips. Ca. 1870.*

*A rare collector's piece cast in copper and decorated with enameled flowers. American. Ca. 1920.*

*Pornographic nude on reverse of frog. American.*

*A doorstop reminiscent of the enchanting Jenny Lind. American. Ca. 1890.*

*Austrian boy. Very unusual full form, detailed model.*

*Cast-iron frog with nude on reverse side. Ca. 1830.*

25. *A doorstop reminiscent of the enchanting Jenny Lind. Last quarter of the 1800s.*

*26. Traditional Buddha conceived with beguiling originality. Circa 1900.*

*Orientalia*

By the 1890s the figural doorstop was still essentially of high Victorian motifs. The Orientalia movement was to affect at least some of the doorstops designed during the latter part of the Victorian period.

Since the opening of Japan to Westerners took place in the 1850s, it was quite natural that Japanese art forms would enjoy increasing popularity in America and Europe. In 1876, many decorative arts of the Far East were exhibited at the Philadelphia Centennial Exhibition. Many gifted and prolific Western designers and artists were deeply influenced by the art of Japan.

By the 1880s Orientalia was in vogue, reaching its full impact in the first quarter of the twentieth century. Figural doorstops have often been used as barometers of current tastes and trends; thus, the craze for anything exotic generated the production of the Buddha doorstop. Buddha is sitting in the classical meditation pose and bears the distinguishing marks of Buddha: a topknot, or cranial protuberance; an "urna," or incised circle above the bridge of the wedge-shaped nose; and elongated earlobes. In the line of the lips can be discerned the so-called archaic smile. The lotus, symbol of purity, is also present. Certainly, the artist of this unique piece, in responding to the Oriental mania, never realized the inappropriateness of crafting a religious subject as a doorstop.

*27. Charming brass or iron Chinaman doorstop made for the American market. Circa 1940.*

The popularity of Orientalia lasted into the 1930s. The spirit lingered through the Art Nouveau and Art Deco periods. Orientalia proliferated in such volume that it was sold through trade journals. An example may be located in the *Sears and Roebuck Catalog of 1927,* which advertises a Japanese Kutani china cat. This sleeping feline doorstop was available with white, gold, and black decoration. The piece could be purchased for $3.85.

*Art Nouveau*

By 1900, Art Nouveau reached its zenith. Some designs that proliferated during this time were neo-Greek, with wave patterns, geometric motifs, and stylized animals and birds.

The peacock, possibly more than any other motif, symbolizes the Art Nouveau movement. An expression of this decade was executed by Louis Tiffany. On the eve of World War One he presented an elaborate stag party. Scantily clad dancing girls carried peacocks on their shoulders and served peacocks under glass to male guests.

The peacock doorstop with its highly textured and colorful plumes of

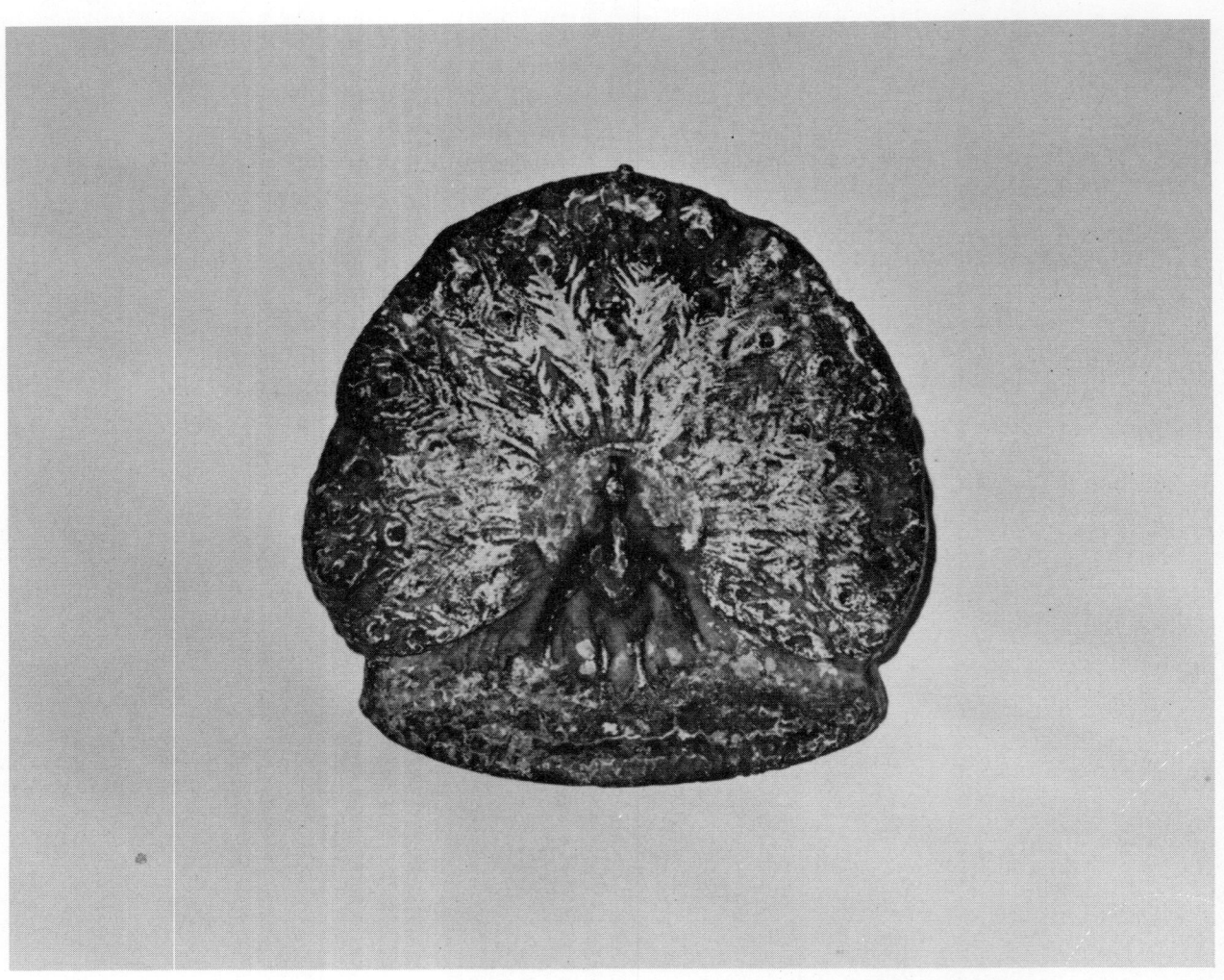

*28. Hard-to-find Art Nouveau peacock. Circa 1910.*

ochre, blue, and green painted on a creme ground typifies this era. The tremendous influence of the Art Nouveau movement dominated the applied arts as much as it did the fine arts, until the outbreak of World War One.

### Art Deco

In the United States the period of Art Deco realized a substantial rise in numbers of figural doorstops. Perhaps the Great Depression added to this growth. People still desired some colorful gaiety to add to a home. For many, large purchases were not feasible; therefore, a small decorative item was chosen. Few objects fit the need more properly than a brightly painted or quaintly sculpted doorstop.

One such Deco object is an enchanting basket of flowers. The motif on the basket is a neat diamond pattern of relief. The flowers are very stylized, as is the entire piece. One may imagine such a stop being used in an interior where corresponding pattern on pattern were utilized. Other weights were elected for the Art Deco period. One such is the patent for a Spanish dancer.

29. *Art Deco basket of stylized flowers.*

30. *Patent Date: November 19, 1929, Design Number: 79,938 Inventor: R.M. Pickard.*

She is definitely reminiscent of the appeal for the Spanish motifs of the time. Two additional stops, although there is little to differentiate them from other 1920 pieces, are baskets of flowers found in the Woodrow Wilson home in Washington, D.C.

One should be aware that many of the stops made in the 1920s and 1930s are copies of older designs, but they are not considered reproductions or fakes. They may be, except for form, entirely different from the stop of 1870. The skillful artist will have modified them in a manner that allows them to be a piece of folk art that should be judged on its own merit. There remain, of course, numerous ones that have no predecessor and are literally small works of sculpting art and ingenious painting — these are ones to be coveted.

## Doorstops After 1935

Dogs in various forms and breeds were especially popular, as the *Sears and Roebuck Catalog of 1938-1939* (Fall-Winter) can attest. For $1.19 one could purchase a cast-metal Bulldog, white with black; a Police Dog, brownish gray; or a Terrier, white brown — all of them included leather leashes.

Ships, covered wagons, cats, horses, sunbonnet babies, and lovely ladies in

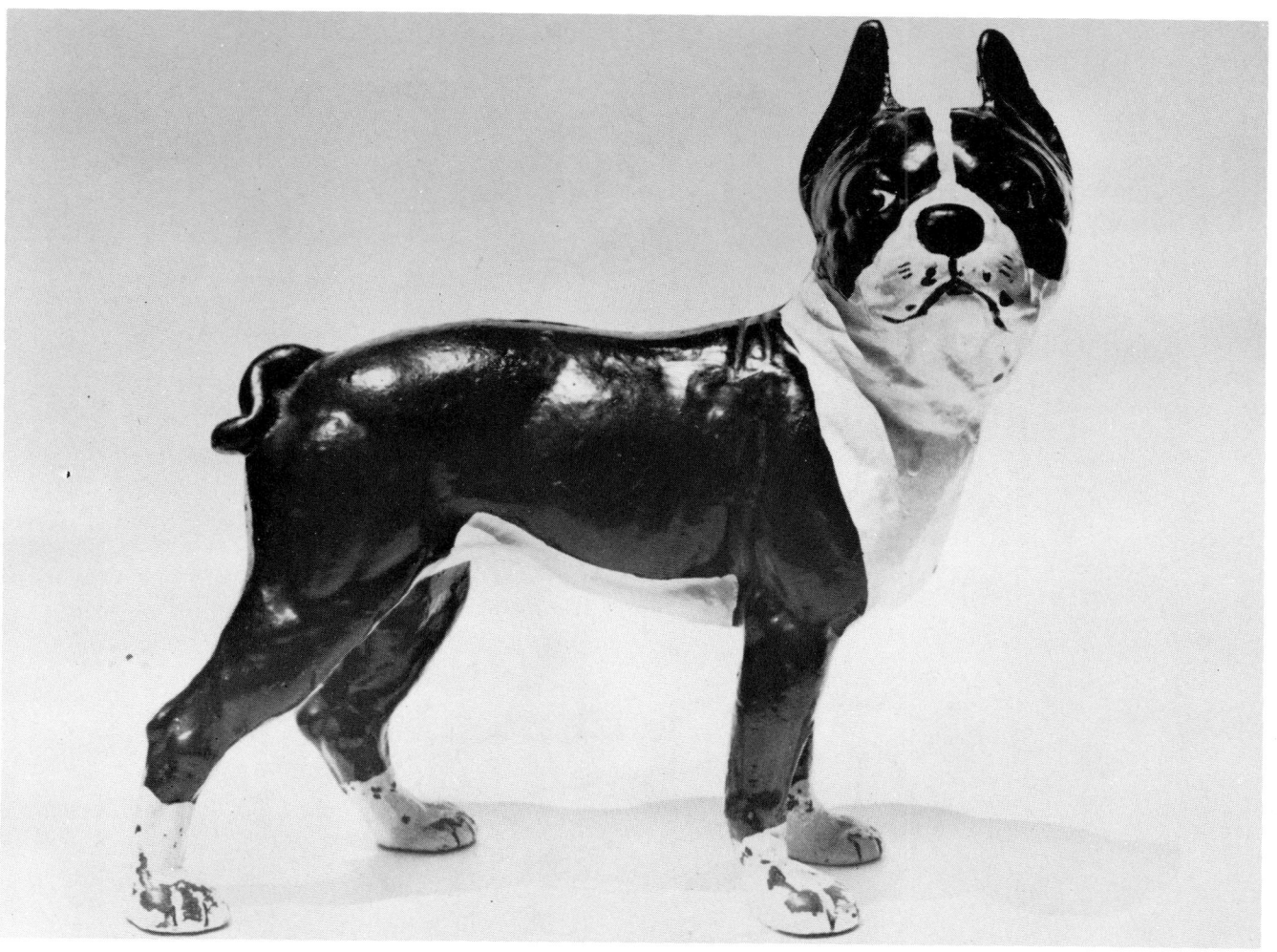

*31. 1938-39 Sear's Catalog offered this Boston Terrier.*

brass or cast-iron were popular subjects for doorstops. A few innovative pieces such as Popeye the sailor and other cartoon characters are found.

By the end of the 1930s we find a transitional figural doorstop being made from hard rubber. The popular ship of 1930 was produced in rubber and attractively painted. These figural rubber pieces were probably short-lived because of the ultimate scarcity of rubber during World War Two.

Composition materials, syroco being the most popular, were used for doorstops in 1944. A Scotty Dog advertised by *Sears and Roebuck Catalogs* exhibits fine detail and workmanship. He is painted black, wears a red collar, and peers through sparkling glass eyes.

Doorstops of this period were often projects undertaken by boys in manual-training classes throughout the United States. Usually these were crudely machine-carved animals or flower baskets. Many of them were painted by the boy. A unique piece that was cast in a Washington, D.C., school district during the 1930s is a bronze frog. Although cast frogs are not exceptional, the fact that this piece is in bronze adds to its charm.

Two flower baskets are pictured. One is a 1975 casting of the other. The new piece was cast of aluminum.

32. *Unusual cast-iron monkey doorstop—tail design supports door. Circa 1930.*

33. *Vividly painted cast-iron Popeye doorstop—freestanding. Circa 1935.*

34. Made prior to World War II, this rubber boat doorstop is a unique find.

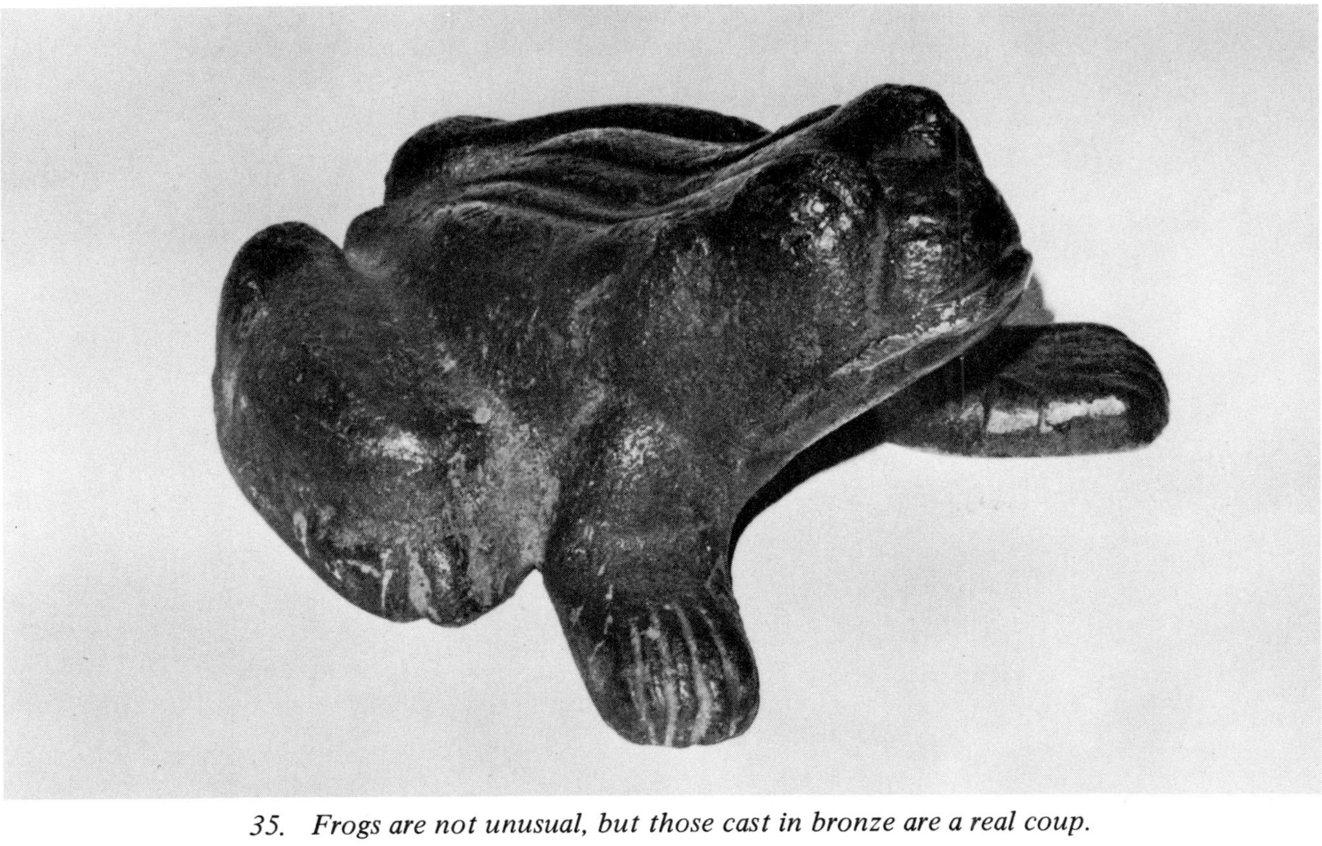

35. Frogs are not unusual, but those cast in bronze are a real coup.

*36. Right basket was cast from basket on left in 1975 manual-arts class. Note difference in size.*

Today's doorstops have degenerated into rubber and wooden wedges. The figural doorstop is perhaps a by-gone only to the generation born after the 1940s. But it provides a typical example of how a useful article gets pushed into the background by new developments in the methods of performing the job it did. Gone are the days when a woodcarver unbridled his mind, drew from his experiences, and created a pattern to be used for a doorstop. Many nineteenth- and early twentieth-century doorstops may be thought as triumphs of the sculptor's art. The attractive design was, in the best examples, molded with great expertise, and the results were often minor works of art. The doorstop, in most instances, provides a candid glimpse of our heritage through its unique subject matter.

# 2
# *A Short History of Iron Manufacture*

*Early Iron Manufacture*

A discussion of the manufacture of doorstops may give the reader a broad view of the history and techniques of an iron foundry. Certain processes of iron casting have been well documented and are readily available to those who pursue detailed information. However, in order to appreciate more fully the aesthetic forms of doorstops it is necessary to understand some of the basic principles. One word of caution: doorstops, at least in the United States, were not thought of as one of the better contributions of the ironmongers. Although fine work is found, most doorstops were an end-of-the-day diversion. The objective is to appreciate the artistic beauty and not the expertise of the foundryman. Considering the traditions and influences of the nineteenth century, it may readily be perceived that the doorstop fits into the category of folk art and not fine art.

These cast-iron doorstops were produced by transient local foundries and were sometimes of marginal quality. This was especially true of the pre-twentieth-century era. Doorstops were, at best, but a small percent of any foundry yield and were, in all probability, executed by small jobbing plants when and as possibilities of sales arose. Because of manufacturing techniques of doorstops, the wooden patterns and resulting molds allowed for easy duplication of these pieces; thus, there are few one-of-a-kind items in this type of iron work. Transportation dictated the area over which foundry products were sold — this fact remained true until the full emergence of the railroad, circa 1870; thus, no foundryman would cast more doorstops, if he cast any at all, than could be sold in the immediate area, since this was not an item of great commercial value. Unless a particular doorstop made a name for itself, or a foundry embossed its trademark on the piece, in all probability there would be no reason to remember the name of the foundry that produced it. At the same time, during the nineteenth century, designs were stolen and reproduced at will.

37. *A rare collector's piece cast in copper. Circa 1920.*

Concisely stated, the term *casting* may be defined as a metal object manufactured by pouring molten metal into a mold that has a pattern or cavity made in the desired shape or design of the object to be produced. The metal is then allowed to solidify inside this cavity. This procedure was introduced four thousand years before Christ. The beginning probably occurred somewhere north of the Black Sea in present-day Russia.

The first metal to undergo this metamorphosis was most likely copper, as archaeologists have discovered molds that prove early man cast spearheads from it. Because it may be used in a pure state, no alloy was required for copper. Another attribute of copper is its ability to be shaped by heating and hammering.

The victories that the Eurasians celebrated as they invaded Mesopotamia several thousand years previous to the birth of Christianity were due to the fact that they had mastered the production of metal weapons. In this land, an early foundryman, presumably by accident, started a high forge fire and discovered the art of copper casting.

Sometime after, a small amount of tin was added to copper, and bronze was produced. The earliest-known cast pieces were elementary forms, such as spearheads, axes, and simple farming tools.

The Eurasian man lived in migratory tribes. He would most often build a furnace by digging a hole in the earth, line it with clay, and when the projects were finished he would move on. As populations became more stablized permanent furnaces were built.

The first record of Chinese iron-casting dated about 600 B.C., and by the seventh century A.D. they were producing many ornamental and useful items. It is not difficult to find examples of their skilled work in the museums of today. The Egyptian cast-bronze cat of the seventh century B.C. does not look that different from the 1930 cast-iron cat produced in the United States — both have the aristocratic expression of felines of all the centuries. It would be unfair to state that these early peoples of the Orient and Egypt had any ideas that the technical processes of casting might encompass the doorstop of the 1900s. But the same skills required of the Chinese, the Egyptian, and others before them are identical to those required for the casting of the later doorstops.

Casting had been an expensive method. But by 1730, technology had advanced enough to enable one Abraham Darby of Coalbrookdale, England, to discover that coke could be used successfully as a fuel. Previously, the stoking of a foundry required a large abundance of wood as fuel. The use of coke cut the manufacturing costs by two-thirds; thus, coke became instrumental to the iron industry.

*American Foundries*

In the colonies, the first successful American foundry was established in 1642. It became known as the Sangus Iron Works of Massachusetts. The Sangus River was close by, and the ore from that area was particularly suitable for the production of iron objects. The famous Sangus Pot, a three-legged kettle with handles and lid, was the first known casting produced in the New World. Many iron plantations were later founded in the piedmont area of Pennsylvania. This area was well suited to the development of many large and small foundries. Bog iron was abundant and readily accessible, and there was plenty of virgin timber for fuel. Mount Joy Forge, commonly known as Valley Forge, was one of these. Others include Hopewell Furnace, Mary Anne, Amy, and Rachel. The latter three are the names of small furnaces that sprouted around the countryside. Many of the small ones were named after the foundryman's wife. Unfortunately, many of them have disappeared because of fire or financial reverses.

It is remarkable that any part of the original foundries is left because of the constant danger of fire. The average furnace had a fire burning constantly. It was considered a routine matter for a spark to ignite the contents. Many places kept buckets of water to douse the flames. More often it became a race to put the water in the bucket to use or consider oneself lucky to escape with life intact.

Small foundries are especially important to the study of doorstops. The reason is that it was here that much of our early folk art and trinket work evolved. It appears that many of the small foundries of the late 1800s and early 1900s made trinket ware, particularly doorstops. Wilton Foundry, Hubley Manufactures, Palmyra-Camden Foundry, and Brunnerville Foundry were a few that produced "ting-a-ling."

Trinket work was the name given to items such as doorstops, trivets, or bells that were small enough to be carried in a bag. Because of the jingling noise they emit, one may hear this category of casting referred to as "ting-a-ling." Many such articles of this type were produced — not the epitome of the ironmonger's best, but in many instances they are certainly his most interesting. Frequently, these items were never meant to be sold but were merely amusing advertising gimmicks to be presented to customers.

From early times through the nineteenth century it would not be unusual, especially in Pennsylvanian barns, to find small iron figures cast in the shape of cows. These were talismen for the farmer; they were intended to be used to chase fire and pestilence from the barns. One could often see them hanging next to the barn door to speed bad spirits on their way.

As stated earlier, the methods for casting doorstops did not vary much from the casting of the first crude spearhead. In truth, all metals are cast in the same manner. The difference is mainly in the temperature of the fire and the medium of the pattern. Iron requires a hotter or higher temperature to melt than does copper or aluminum.

Most early 1800s furnaces were built into the side of a hill. Ore, charcoal, and limestone would be poured continuously into the top of the stack. The melted ore would pour out onto the floor of the hearth. The floor was usually covered with sand, the substance from which castings were formed. A foundryman would mold or make the desired shape in the sand. Generally, the design was a channel from the furnace to a center pool or oblong shape. At right angles to this center, or "sow," were smaller channels. They were called "pigs." Pigs were split from the sow; hence, the term "pig iron." Later, the sow would also be broken into appropriate portions. These pigs and sows would be sold to the blacksmith for his forging work.

Occasionally, a more artistic foundryman, if time and inclination allowed, would make one of the pig molds into a fanciful shape — this process may have caused many early toys and trinkets to develop. When furnaces became more permanent structures, as the Cornwall Furnace in Pennsylvania, the molten iron would be caught in large buckets and poured or ladled into the desired molds. This was dangerous work. More than one foundryman suffered severe burns or lost his life in this wretched task.

Cast-iron and brass doorstops were products made by regional jobbing foundries. A master woodcarver or pattern maker would be commissioned by the foundry to carve a pattern to be used as a doorstop. From this wood pattern a white lead metal casting would be made. At this point in production the signature of the carver, the foundry's name or hallmark, the date, and the design pattern number would be embossed. Once a master pattern had been created, endless duplicates could readily be produced at low cost to the foundry.

*Casting*

It is not the purpose of this book to enter into a detailed discussion of actual sand-casting methods, but a brief description may be helpful to the collector.

Doorstops may be classified into three groups as far as method of manufacture is concerned.

For a figural doorstop the elected pattern is laid flat on a broad piece of wood or follow board. Moist sand, usually a high-grade silica, is rammed tightly around the pattern. The ramming of sand makes it possible for the mold to retain its shape. More sand is added until this medium is level with the top of the drag flask. Another board is placed on the level area, and the entire drag flask is completely rolled over. The pattern or follow board is removed. The underside of the pattern is once again exposed. After a careful placement of a gating arrangement to allow the molten metal to flow into the cavity, the pattern is removed. Now the metal may be poured into the cavity. When this process has been completed the iron casting is removed, the sand particles brushed from it, and then filed and finished. The above method could be used for a flat or solid-back casting.

A more complicated method is to use a cope and drag. The cope flask is merely the reverse of a drag flask. It is set on top of the bottom flask. In addition, it must have sprue and riser pins. The sprue and riser are inserted for the purpose of pouring and facilitating the escape of gases. Now the metal may be poured into the cavity. The method employing the cope and drag might produce the full mold or a hollow back. Of the three styles, the full-mold method is generally the most expensive. In America, many early nineteenth-century doorstops of this type were made in the foundries in the Shenandoah Valley.

Another doorstop form that imparts the appearance of a full-form figure is one with a rivet or screw. It utilizes two sets of cope and drag. The front and the back of the figure are molded separately. After casting, the two pieces are joined together by a rivet. A rivet is a metal bolt with a head on one end, used to fasten the sections together. The rivet is inserted through a drilled hole. The plain end is then blunted so it will not pull out. The interior of this doorstop is hollow and, therefore, may be lighter in weight than would be expected from its appearance.

38. Left to right: elephant is full form; flower basket is flat back; sitting terrier is riveted together with a screw.

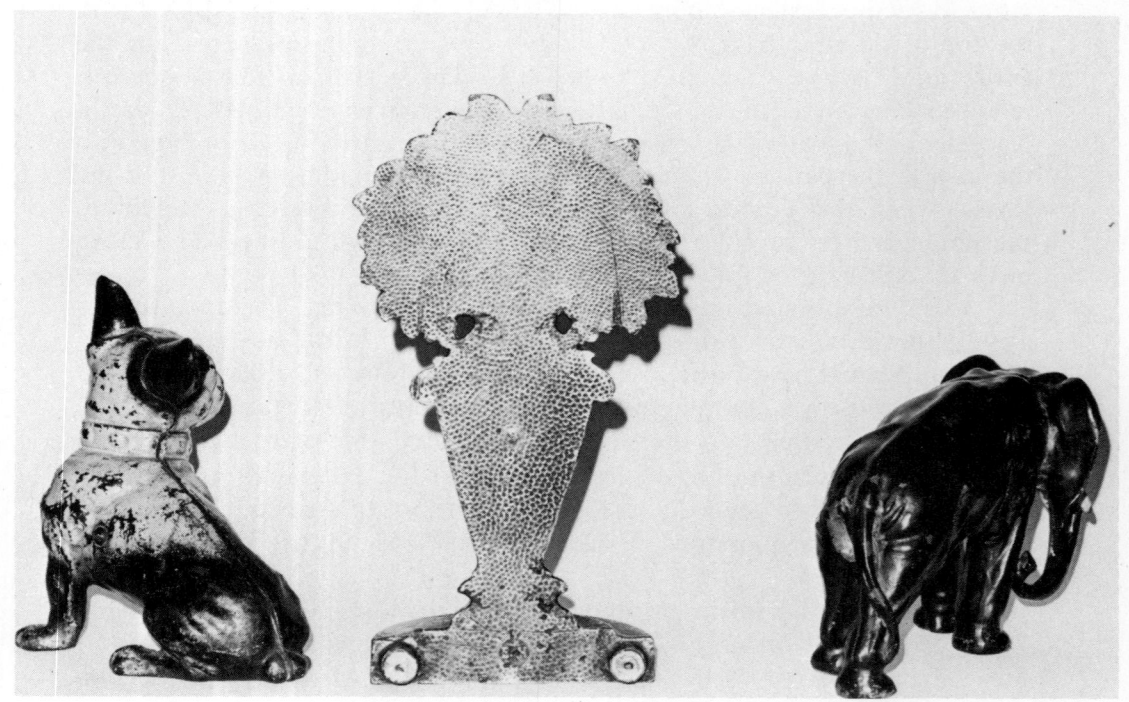

39. Left to right: reverse of the above three doorstops.

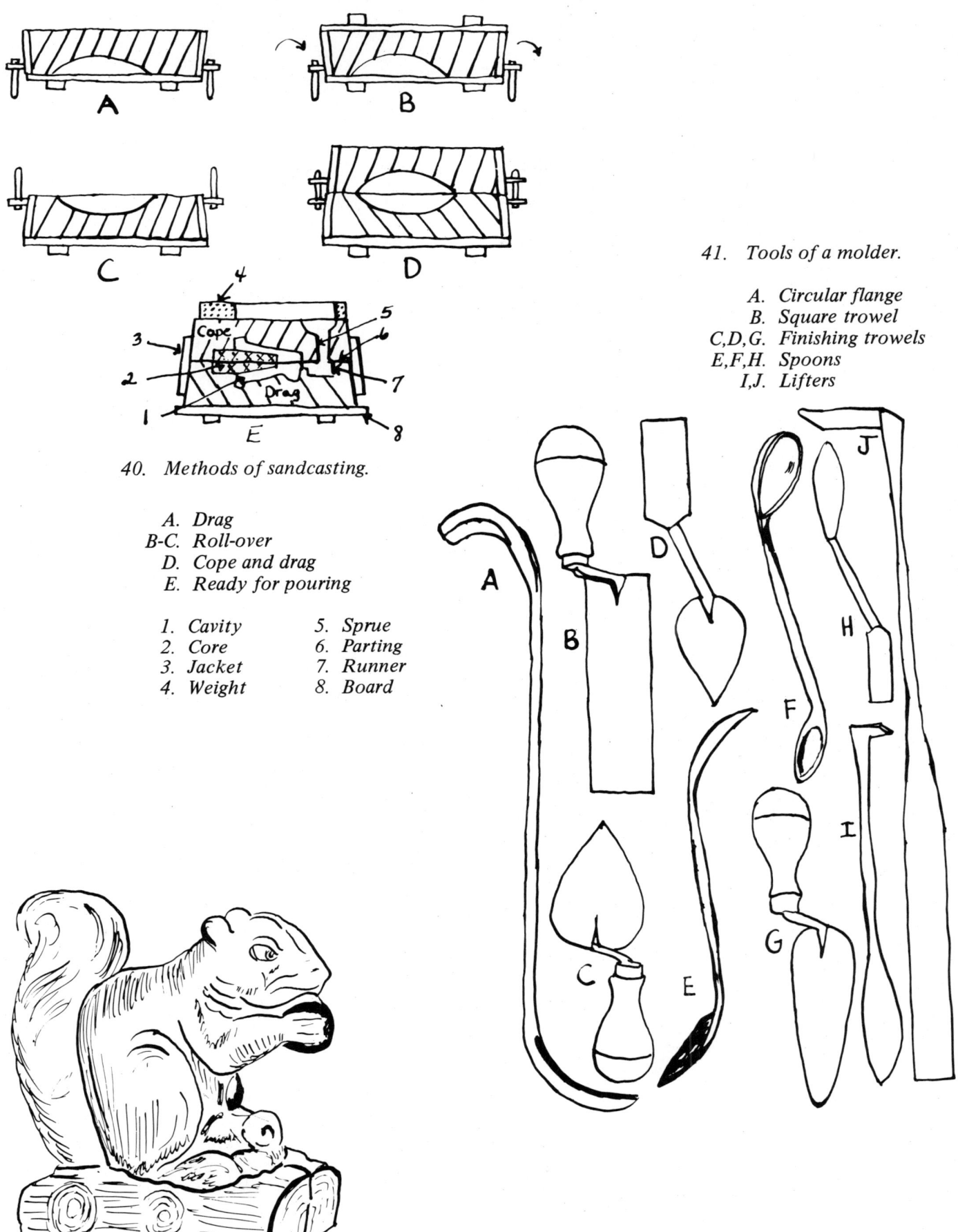

40. Methods of sandcasting.

    A. Drag
  B-C. Roll-over
    D. Cope and drag
    E. Ready for pouring

1. Cavity     5. Sprue
2. Core       6. Parting
3. Jacket     7. Runner
4. Weight   8. Board

41. Tools of a molder.

    A. Circular flange
    B. Square trowel
 C,D,G. Finishing trowels
 E,F,H. Spoons
   I,J. Lifters

42. American squirrel doorstop—typical full-form casting from the Shenandoah Valley. Circa 1920.

*43. Cast-iron black bear from Virginia, showing a rivet.*

### The Woodcarver

Metal casting is dependent on the woodcarver. It is the carver who must be able to visualize or imagine what the finished product will be. He must be skilled not only in woodcarving but also must know the fundamental principles of casting. He also must be versed in various aspects, strengths, weaknesses, and peculiarities of the metal.

Most woodcarvers, or pattern makers as they are now called, would pick a particular wood for its properties, depending on its eventual utilization. Generally, the three pines are northern white pine, Idaho pine, and sugar pine. Sometimes Central American or Mexican mahogany might be used.

As stated earlier, casting really belongs to the woodcarver. The woodcarvers of the nineteenth century are often synonymous with folk art. Their designs are seldom a true rendition of real life. However, they are able to incorporate a large amount of detail into the design; therefore, we are able to recognize the figure not from the object outline as much as from the details. A finished product is a desired, not perfect, duplication. An early woodcarver usually did not have the discipline nor opportunity to follow through on the studies of anatomy or botanical structure; hence, a whimsical style developed for most figural doorstops.

It may be necessary to study the style of these cast doorstops to understand the foregoing explanation. Even though they are related through the riches of folk art there are considerable differences; for example, a rose is easily distinguishable in a basket of flowers. Yet, no two roses are exactly alike. Some are rather flat specimens, others have three or four carefully outlined petals, while still others have close attention paid to the inside details of a full-blown rose.

The above pictures show flower baskets containing poppies. One, the

44. Two signed *HUBLEY* doorstops.

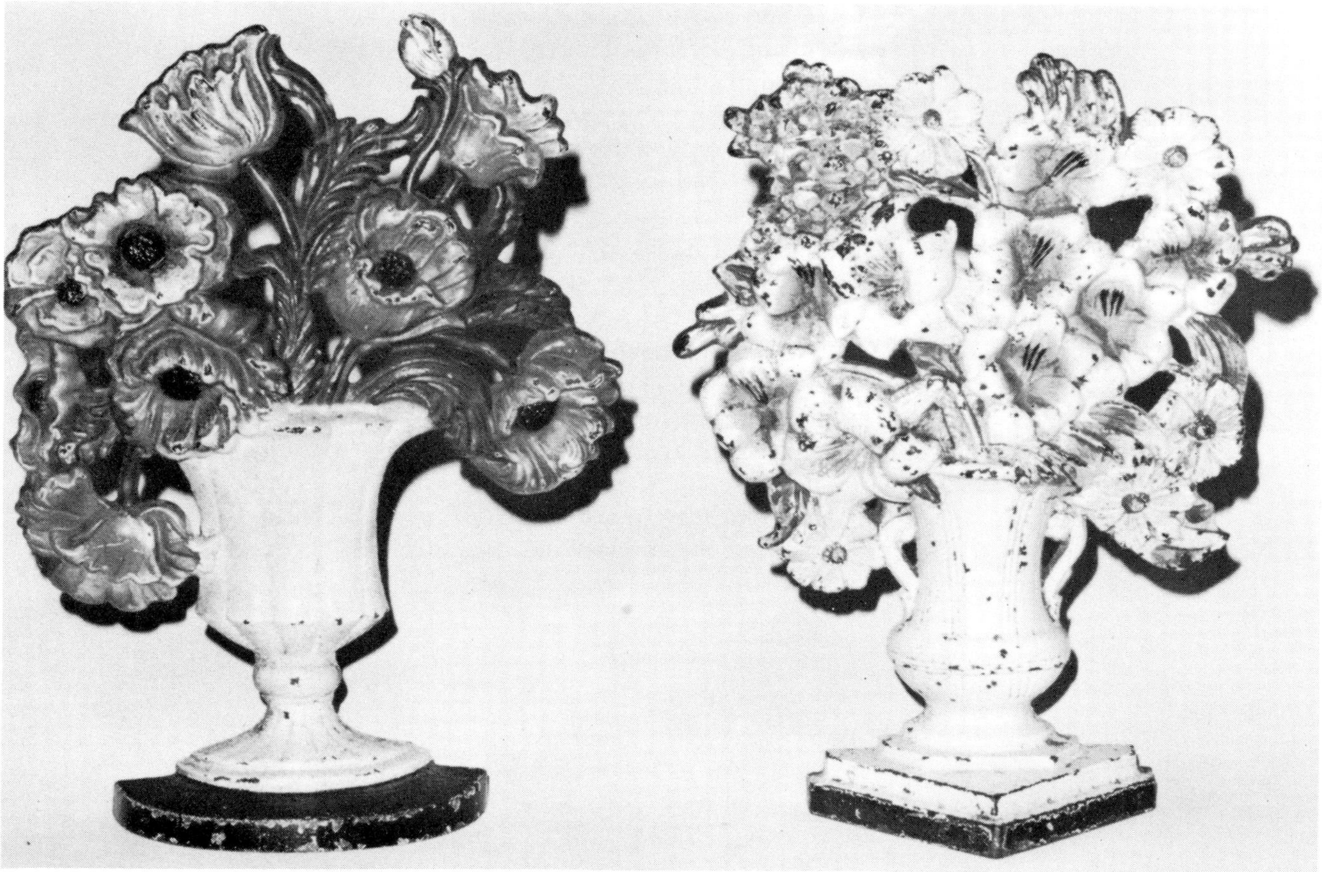

45. Example of late doorstop. Note difference in technique from *HUBLEY* basket in previous photograph.

smaller, was made by the Hubley Company and is exquisitely painted. But even without paint there could be little doubt, to the casual observer, that the basket contains poppies. A larger doorstop, entirely different, maker unknown, also holds an abundant bouquet of the same flowers. Its lines are finer, the flowers and leaves are bigger and more carefully defined. There are more deeply cut lines to show the ruffling abilities of a poppy. Yet both baskets suggest the luxuriousness of the poppy blossom.

The union of the art of the woodcarver and the technical abilities of the foundryman was a beautiful mergence. From that mergence came a delightful folk-art product: the cast-iron figural doorstop.

### Surface Decoration

Discovering a doorstop with its original finish of japanned lacquer, paint, or bronze powder is a lucky find. More often the former luster of the piece will have vanished from years of use, being replaced by the almost forgotten glow of the black leading.

Most American foundries dipped the finished doorstop in large vats of red or black japanned lacquer, then allowed them to dry by suspending them over large drain boards. The more carefully dried pieces would not have paint runs on them. When detailed painting was desired, the doorstops were given to local ladies to hand decorate.

The women often painted the pieces in bright, naturalistic colors of their own choosing. Eventually, the foundries color-coded the pieces to establish greater control and standardization; thus, in the nineteenth century, painting was primarily a cottage industry with no definite color guidelines established by the foundry. Some earlier cast-iron stops before 1850 were vividly but fleetingly painted. By the mid-Victorian period there emerged many bold and elaborately hand-painted pieces; thus, the decoration of the doorstop varies from pure black, with no color trim, to careful enameling in many hues. If the stop was sold with only the black lacquer, the purchaser quite often would paint the doorstop according to his own likes.

The Virginia Metalcrafters coat their cast-iron doorstops with a red primer, followed by a coat of sprayed black-lacquer paint. If a more elaborate color scheme is desired, they use employees in various other departments, such as shipping, to hand paint according to a standardized color guide. Earlier in the history of this foundry they also used local women to paint their decorative ironwork.

Later doorstops are often spray painted instead of hand done. The change from good careful handwork to the frenzy of mass-production spray painting was accomplished in, remarkably, a few years.

Paint on a cast-iron doorstop often adds great decorative charm to the piece, but one should remember that untrimmed doorstops also have age and personality.

46. *Sheaves of wheat in cast-iron, with only black japanning for a coating.*

# 3
# Patents, Trademarks, and Reproductions

*Patents*

Because of the piracy of various designs, the British government formalized a system of registering parcels. This system granted protection to the designer or inventor of wares for a designated period of time.

47. *Jumbo the Elephant English doorporter—registered 18 May 1882. Rare.*

A British Patent Office diamond-shaped registration device occurs on Victorian wares from 1842 through 1883. The purpose of this mark was to show that the design or shape had been registered with the Patent Office in London and was thus protected from being stolen by another manufacturer. One example of a doorporter bearing this device is the cast-iron elephant Jumbo, a popular animal celebrity exhibited by the P.T. Barnum circus during the later part of the nineteenth century. Jumbo gained such notoriety

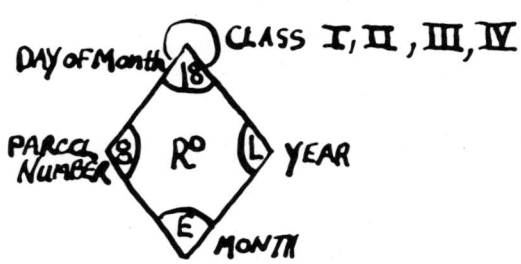

48. *This type of diamond registration mark was used by the English Patent Office from 1868-1883.*

that many commercial items were produced in his likeness. The elephant doorporter is of cast-iron, with a brightly painted harness, and bears the name JUMBO embossed on its plinth. Its diamond registration mark may be interpreted as 18 May 1882.

From January 1884 to January 1909, registered designs were consecutively numbered, and these numbers appear on wares with the prefix "Rd" or "Rd No."

One engaging doorporter bearing the British registration number imprinted on the back reads "*Rd No* 2812239." Barely visible on the front is the title DOC JIM. The weight was registered between January 1896 and January 1897. Sir Leander Starr Jameson (1853-1917) was a British colonial statesman who was educated in the medical profession. He was instrumental in obtaining concessions from Lobengula, which ultimately led to the formation of the British South Africa Company. Though sometimes impulsive and overconfident, "Dr. Jim" was extremely popular for his charm, intelligence, and selflessness. Jameson's work toward racial harmony and his material progress in South Africa were proof of his patriotic spirit. Jameson was affectionately called "Doc Jim" by the British populace.

The United States Patent Office files, design division, contain under eighty varied doorstop innovations. Only about eleven of these are actual figural designs. Others are of the rubber-tipped, screw-in-the-wall type, or a variation thereof.

The importance of the patent lies not so much in the fact that patents exist but that there are so few; yet, there are literally hundreds of figural doorstop designs available. Maybe many of the original designers did not undertake the lengthy problem of patenting a particular doorstop. It was common knowledge that the doorstop production was somewhat of a free game and, therefore, whatever the market fancied, the foundry made. There existed little reason to bother with a patent design, as most designs were readily borrowed or outright stolen. One speculation for few patents is that these stops were folk objects and, therefore, classified as minisculpture. Sculpture and folk art are seldom patented. Another reason may be that one had to hire an attorney to do a patent search. Money was not always available for such ventures.

Among the designs that were patented, one may find a charming dwarf with a lantern, a Spanish dancer, a Colonial man, two coaches with horses, a flower basket, an appealing spotted dog with a tilted head, and a little Dutch girl.

49. *Doc Jim so endeared himself to the British populace that they designed a doorporter of him in 1896.*

The patents have long expired on these stops. The earliest, a Dutch girl, dates from 1916. Obviously, floor antiques were made prior to that date but bear little or no record of their origin (see Appendix).

A spring bouquet is gaily represented in a flower basket designed and patented by Mabel Harlow. The patent was granted 21 March 1916. A delicate blue shades the lattice-work holder. Pink crocuses, yellow daffodils, and perky narcissus are well defined. This array is surrounded with bleeding hearts, forget-me-nots, and periwinkle. How enchanting to find this 4¼-inch base, 6½-inch tall reminder of springtime. The back of this particular doorstop has a hollowed-out casting.

Another (patent date 28 October 1930) is a fantastic creation by Charles Tuteur. A full-form figure of two horses, a coach complete with passenger, and two coachmen are elaborately detailed. The coach is painted yellow and red and is imprinted with the words LONDON MAIL. The driver is a portly sort, dressed in green with a yellow top hat. The horses with bobbed tails appear to be objecting to their task. The coachman is wearing a swallow-tail

50. *Reverse of Doc Jim doorporter.*

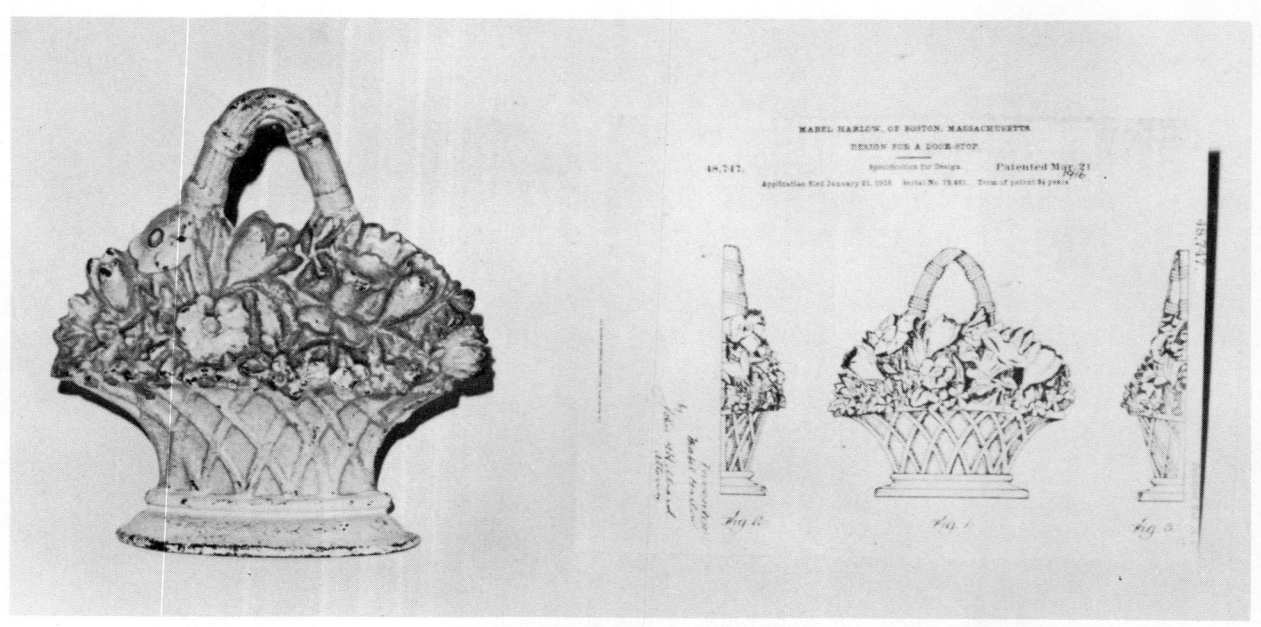

*51. Flower basket with patent.*

coat. The work is so delicately defined that it is possible to perceive button holes on one side of the casting and see the buttons on the other. The passenger remains obscure, but one is quite able to detect a wig on this personage.

The doorstop itself is narrow, barely 1¼ inches in width. Because of the narrow width it was necessary to place two lips, one on each back wheel, to ensure an upright stance for the doorstop.

*52. Coach and patent design.*

## Trademarks

As early as 1865 trade catalogues offered doorstops, handles, and other diversified items. However, it is almost impossible to trace the exact age of most American doorstops unless there was a patent date or a foundry trademark on the piece. Pre-twentieth-century designs were pirated from one foundry to another, and often the foundry's name was never embossed on the doorstop.

One typical reason for unsigned doorstops is the "end-of-the-day" manufacture. Molten iron that was left over from the foundry's main production work was seldom wasted. To consume the metal, men would frequently cast several figural doorstops. Many early foundries that produced doorstops cast stove parts as their main manufacturing line. These doorstops were sometimes commissioned by the townspeople, sold to local buyers, or taken home as gifts. Occasionally, end-of-the-day manufactured doorstops were embossed with a trademark, as is the case of St. Louis Malleable, St. Louis, Missouri. This foundry produced a cast-iron frog and a full-form, core-molded Aunt Jemima that were given away as favors and advertisement pieces.

Frequently, a number is embodied on the back of a doorstop — this number refers to the pattern design used by the foundry. It does not indicate age or give a clue to the name of the foundry that produced it. A few doorstops were signed, but the majority were not. Some of the names and marks that may be found include: HUBLEY; FOUNDRY COLDWATER, MICH; NEWARK, N.J.; S; RIFE-LOTH CORP; WILTON, WRIGHTSVILLE, PA.; GREENBLATT STUDIOS, 1924; and, VA. METALCRAFTERS hallmark.

*53. Hallmark of Virginia Metalcrafters.*

The Virginia Metalcrafters are still utilizing the original wood patterns that were used for the earlier stops. There exists a Boxer dog inscribed with D.S.W. (David S. Weaver) 1939. Presumably Mr. Weaver designed the pattern for this piece. Although little is known of most pattern carvers, the name Calvin Roy Kinstler of Baltimore, Maryland, is known. Mr. Kinstler carved patterns of a famous line of thoroughbred horses.

The following equine doorstops were produced from the original wooden patterns: Citation, unmarked except for Virginia Metalcrafters hallmark on the reverse side, found in brass and cast-iron; Hunter, name embossed on front, hallmark on reverse side, black cast-iron; and King's Genius, name embossed on front, hallmark on reverse side, black cast-iron. It should be noted that these three pieces should always have the Virginia Metalcrafters hallmark on the reverse side, unless the unscrupulous take one and deliberately remove the hallmark prior to making a new casting. King's Genius in brass, bearing the earlier name of the Rife-Loth Corporation, later known as Virginia Metalcrafters, Waynesboro, Virginia, may still be found. Any piece bearing the original name of the company would be older than one bearing Virginia Metalcrafters hallmark.

Other original wood patterns from the same firm are: a German Shepherd called "Buddy" patented 1929 and not in production today; Irish Setter patented 1947; Cocker Spaniel in the likeness of "Dreamboy," 1949. The dogs were all cast of iron. There was also a fox head and whip doorstop. It is found cast entirely in brass or with a black cast-iron head and brass whip handle. The above doorstops, except for Buddy, are in production today and will bear the Virginia Metalcrafters hallmark.

As stated earlier, unless a particular doorstop made a name for itself, there would be no reason to remember the name of the foundry that produced it. Very rarely were doorstops signed by their makers. In the same context, it is virtually impossible to distinguish the American product from the English counterpart unless there is an identifying mark on the piece.

*Reproductions*

Since the end of the fifteenth century, generations of forgers have worked to supply the world with spurious antiques. Doorstops have not been omitted.

Although to some these art forms are not great treasures, they are growing scarcer and more difficult to locate. Reproductions abound on the market, requiring the collector to be wary of each purchase and yet stimulating the need to find the authentic old pieces before they are gone forever. The collector who makes a careful study of the old stops will be able to track down and identify those that may still be hiding from the casual observer. Being aware of the new weights that are produced and sold as old is important to the serious collector.

54. *Early English foxhead doorporter. Circa 1830. (In reproduction.)*

In the strict meaning of the word, a *fake* is an article that is made or an object that is tampered with in order to deceive or receive monetary gain.

There are many doorstops sold in the department stores and elsewhere; however, these are not meant as fakes. These new items are being produced in the United States and abroad. The problem begins when an unknowing or unscrupulous dealer places these same pieces in his shop. Perhaps a sprinkling of saltwater and a few weeks to a month in the sun will grant the proper aging. A bit of banging received by the surface of the doorstop will effectively chip the paint. Presto! a "properly" aged doorstop appears.

Apart from artificial aging wrought with such clever skill, it should not be forgotten that the imitation will also receive signs of genuine wear once it has become second-hand.

Learn the vital signs for differentiating old cast-iron from new. View each potential purchase as a possible forgery, then let the piece prove that it is a valid antique.

Discretion should be administered when two or more of one exact design appear in close proximity. Imitations have a natural inclination to stay together, and if several pieces are coming from the same mold, then there may be something amiss.

The work of the modern iron caster may be betrayed by a routine manner. Often the detail of a doubtful piece will be less refined than the prototype. If a new doorstop is cast from an old weight, the new piece will lose some of the original detail. When another casting is taken from the second doorstop, a little more detail is lost — thus, a third- or fourth-generation casting will possess form but very little detail. As discussed earlier, some of the new pieces are fine reproductions made from the original wood patterns. The best and most authentic reproduction is when a new wooden pattern is carved that copies the old doorstop. In this way no detail is lost, and a perfect-quality piece may be formed down to the most minute detail. One would naturally assume that these newer rivals would be less expensive, but some are priced as high or higher than the originals.

Modern casting sand is frequently coarser than the nineteenth-century mediums; therefore, a pebbled surface is sometimes evident on later pieces. They show marks left from grains of sand. Even when painted, the later doorstop is not as smooth. Aged iron presents a silky surface to the tactile sense.

Oxidation is the scourge of iron; it manifests itself as rust on the surface. The forgers who try to make a reproduction look old often resort to burying a new iron doorstop. When moisture in the ground and iron unite, an orange powdery residue called rust forms. This new rust may appear in blotches on the exterior of unpainted cast-iron. Occasionally, some will rub off, leaving an orange dust on the hand. Old doorstops that have been painted or oiled have little or no surface corrosion. Corrosion on antique doorstops is dark brown. On most new ones the color tends to be more orange.

When rust is evident on an old stop, it usually has formed on the base and has gradually worked upward. The contact between the base and the damp floor begins the oxidation process. Once started, rust will spread even in dry air. Rust on an old specimen shows deeper pitting of the metal. Recently buried items show superficial corrosion. Traces of surface wear should be established, for forgeries generally lack patina; there is always something pristine about the piece. A good basic knowledge of cast-iron may enable the

*55. Note difference in size and detail of an original Punch and the black reproduction. Original: 12¼ inches tall; 9 inches wide. Reproduction: 11¾ inches tall; 8¾ inches wide.*

*56. Reverse of original Punch and the black reproduction.*

collector to better identify the original doorstop from the clever fake.

The specimens should be examined on the base and back. Worn areas develop from normal use.

Earlier doorstop makers often took greater care in their finished product than today's manufacturer. Manufacturing costs must be cut; therefore, by necessity, less handwork is employed on such items. One feature of the early doorstop-maker's work was the painstaking filing of sharp edges. Good, clear definition of a subject is a prerequisite for a prime piece.

On the hollow-back doorstops the reverse side does not retain the detail of the original piece but appears crude, coarse, and pebbly.

Size is also a factor in determining a reproduction. When an old doorstop is used as a pattern, shrinkage of the iron occurs. Cast-iron shrinks approximately one-eighth of an inch per foot; thus, the newer stop will be smaller than the original.

The weight of a doorstop does not necessarily indicate whether the piece is old or new. Frequently, the newer piece is of a higher specification metal than the original. Today, with government regulations, most newer doorstops will be of a higher or better grade of gray iron. The older stops were made from a lesser grade of metal called scrap iron, which had a lower

57. *Examples of one design: one on the left is original; middle is early 1920 model; right is a much later reproduction.*

density; thus, the older specimen may be lighter in weight than its newer rival.

Another reason why reproduction doorstops may weigh more than the original is that detail is lost in each subsequent casting. Areas on the original are usually concave and detailed. On the reproduction casting, these same concave areas are often filled with metal and produce the variance of weight.

Subject matter is a determining factor, in the selection of which doorstops are likely to be reproduced. Weights that have universal appeal, such as cats, dogs, and baskets of flowers, are suitable candidates for modern mass production. On the other hand, a doorporter such as "Doc Jim" has a limited attraction on the American market, and, thus, it is probable it will never be copied.

As is true of many collectibles, prices are escalating; therefore, finding a reasonably priced specimen is becoming a more difficult task. Adding to the challenge is the fact that availability of these doorstops is waning. However, with patience and prudent judgement one may build a pleasing folk-art collection that represents a worthwhile investment.

*A carefully painted original "Punch with Dog." Ca. 1870.*

*A rare "Judy with Baby," sporting bright paint. Ca. 1875.*

*Art Deco basket of stylized flowers. Probably English. Ca. 1915.*

*Regional Victorian flower basket from Brunnerville, Pennsylvania.*

*A distinguished rendition of a fruit basket. A welcome addition to any door. American. Ca. 1910.*

*A large vase full of neatly painted black-eyed Susans. American. Ca. 1925.*

58. Large cat with bow. Reproduction—14¼ inches tall.

# *Appendix*

*Patents*

59. Patent Date: November 26, 1925 Design Number: 79,982 Inventor: R.M. Pickard

60. Patent Date: February 3, 1931   Design Number: 83,223   Inventor: C. Tuteur

61. Patent Date: December 2, 1930   Design Number: 82,682   Inventor: L.J. Laroche

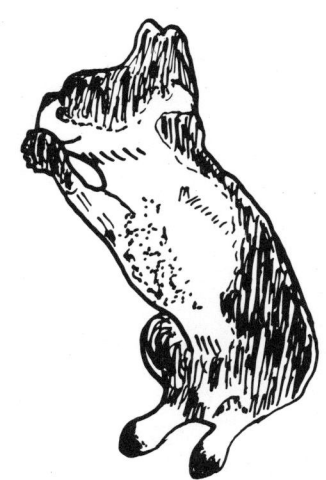

62. Patent Date: January 13, 1931  Design Number: 83,051  Inventor: W. Lauderbach

63. *Patent Date: November 24, 1925 Design Number: 68,848 Inventor: P.J. Bradish*

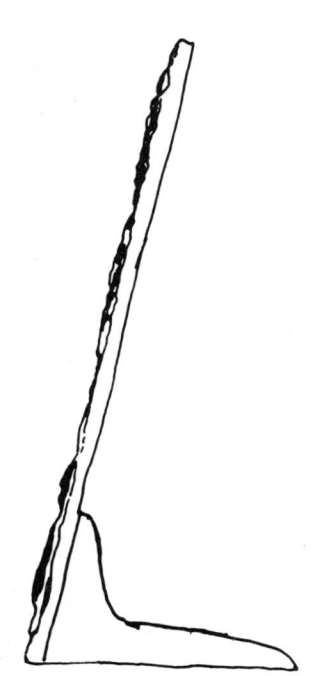

64. *Patent Date: May 9, 1939 Design Number: 114,639 Inventor: E.W. Menger*

65. Patent Date: December 2, 1930 Design Number: 82,654 Inventor: J.W. Barnett

66. Patent Date: October 30, 1923 Design Number: 63,190 Inventor: J.W. McElroy

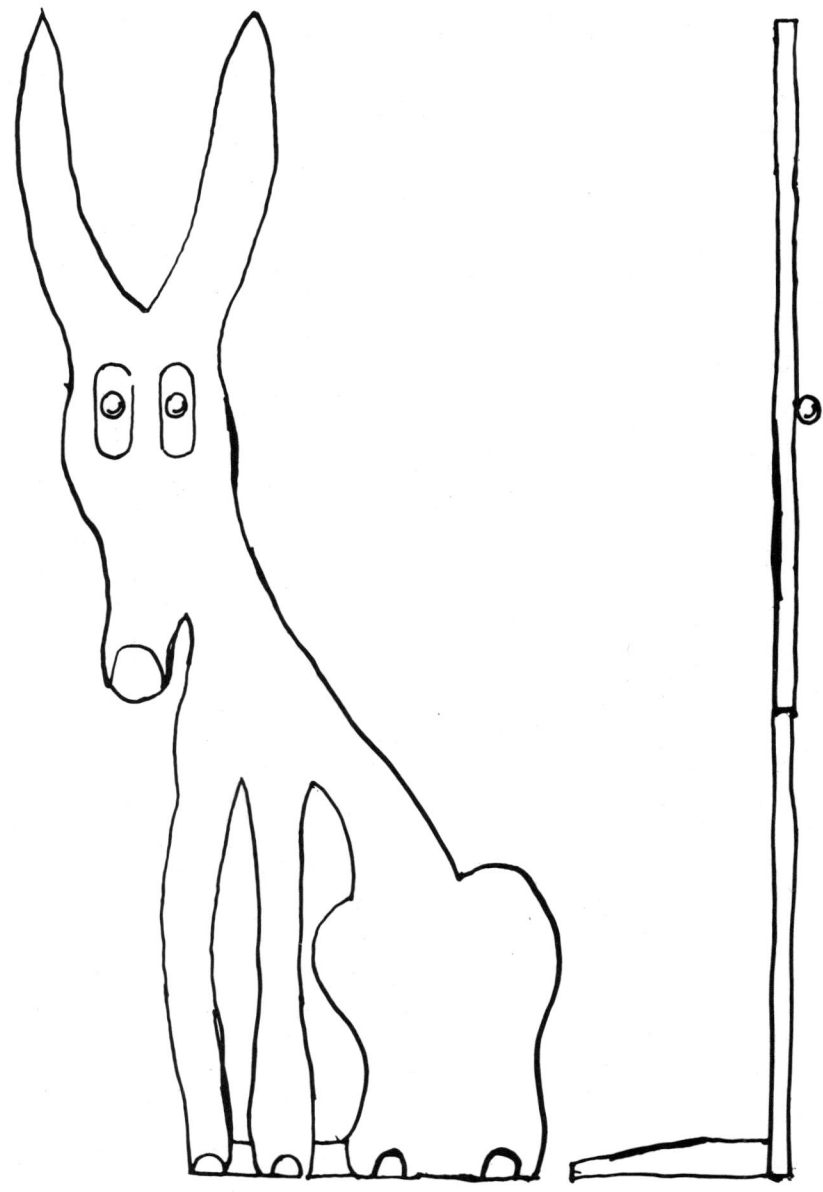

67. *Patent Date: December 4, 1934 Design Number: 93,971 Inventor: L. Clark*

68. *Patent Date: February 15, 1916 Design Number: 48,567 Inventor: M.H. Nevius*

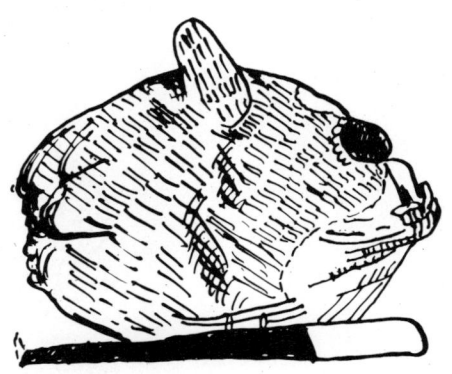

69. Patent Date: December 4, 1928 Design Number: 77,051 Inventor: C. Blow

70. Patent Date: February 15, 1916 Design Number 48,566 Inventor: M.H. Nevius

71. Patent Date: November 19, 1929 Design Number: 79,937 Inventor: R.M. Pickard

# Figural Doorstops

72. *Colorful country rooster. Circa 1940.*

73. *Grape leaves—replica of earlier English doorporter.*

74. *Spanish galleon of cast-iron with copper wash. Circa 1930.*

75. *Round-handled flower baskets with fluted rims, sporting a variety of garden flowers—late Victorian. American.*

76. *Lady with watering can—Regency era, probably English. Fifteen inches tall. Rare.*

77. *Appealing folk-art cat wearing a pink bow.*

78. *Proud cockatoo on perch. Early twentieth century.*

79. Cast-iron invitations of good hospitality. Circa 1910.

80. Largest to smallest baskets in author's collection. Range 5¾ inches to 18 inches.

81. *Unusual mother-daughter doorstops—large one for outside door, and small version fits interior door.*

82. *Lightweight examples of realistic flower motifs.*

83. Typical late 1920s basket of flowers.

84. Another typical late 1920s basket of flowers.

85. Still another example of late 1920s basket of flowers.

86. Scarce iris and unique Easter lily doorstops.

87. *Unusual urn container holding assorted flowers—American.*

88. *Fanciful ribbon-handled flower baskets of Edwardian period— American.*

89. *Spring Miss. Circa 1920.*

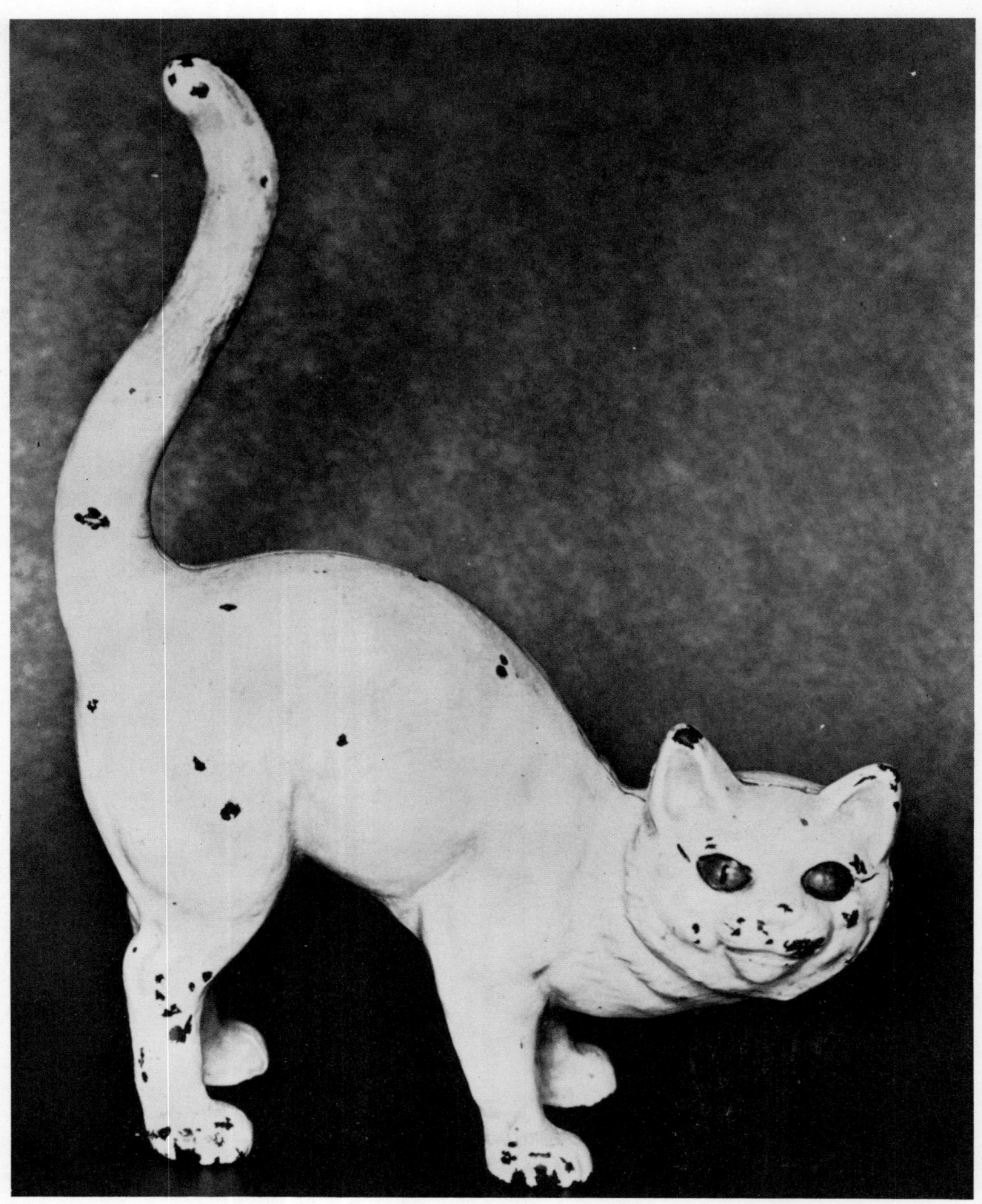
*90. Example of rare naughty cat. Circa 1900.*

91. *Elephant doorstop with trunk designed to be a handle.*

92. *A dainty design of spring flowers. Circa 1925.*

*93. Intriguing cast-iron example of the Mayflower. Circa 1930.*

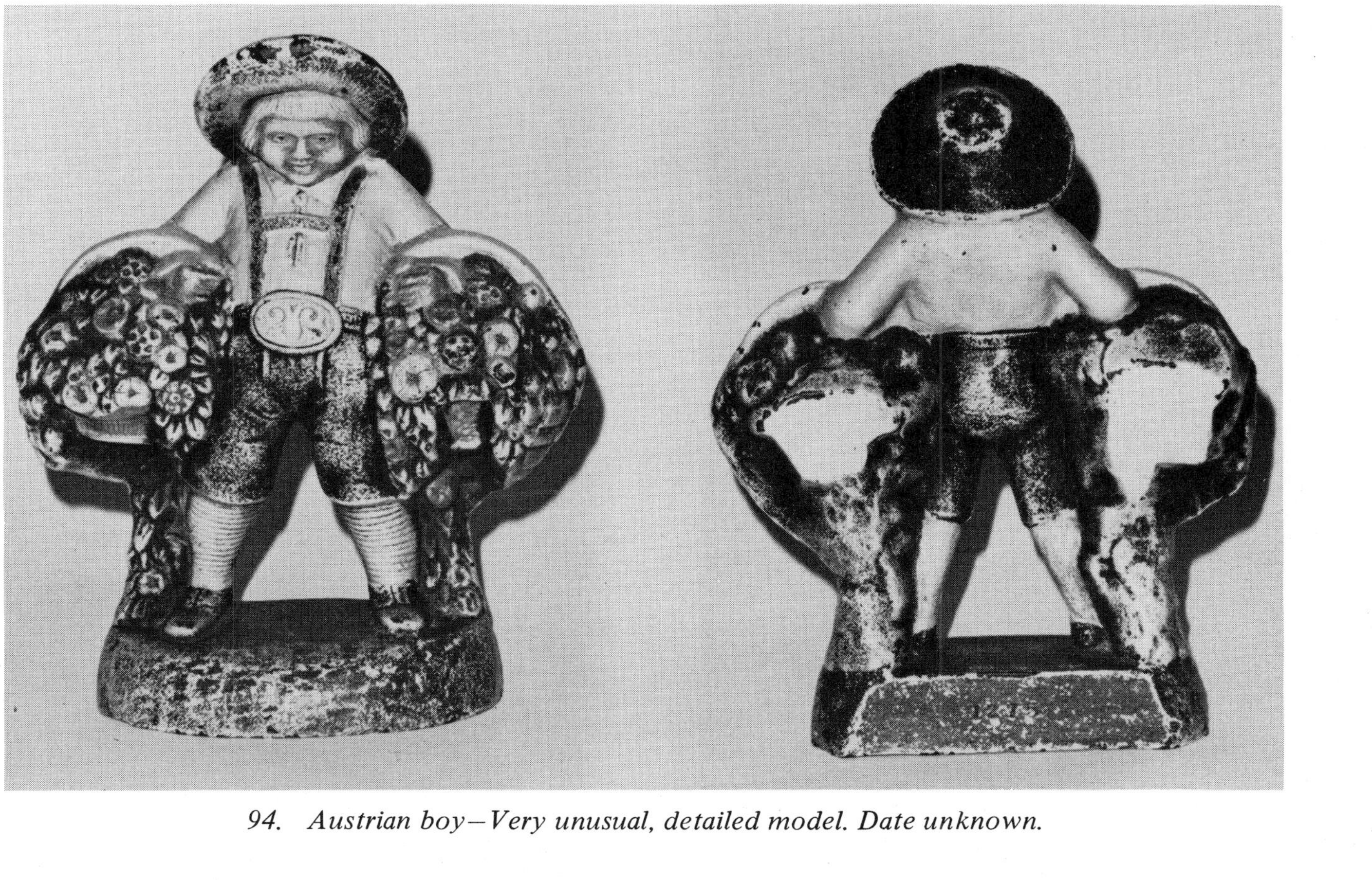

*94. Austrian boy—Very unusual, detailed model. Date unknown.*

95. *Two winning Scotty dogs. Circa 1930.*

96. *Wooden flower basket—typical manual training project.*

97. *Reproduction of Hubley Co. reclining cat. Not signed.*

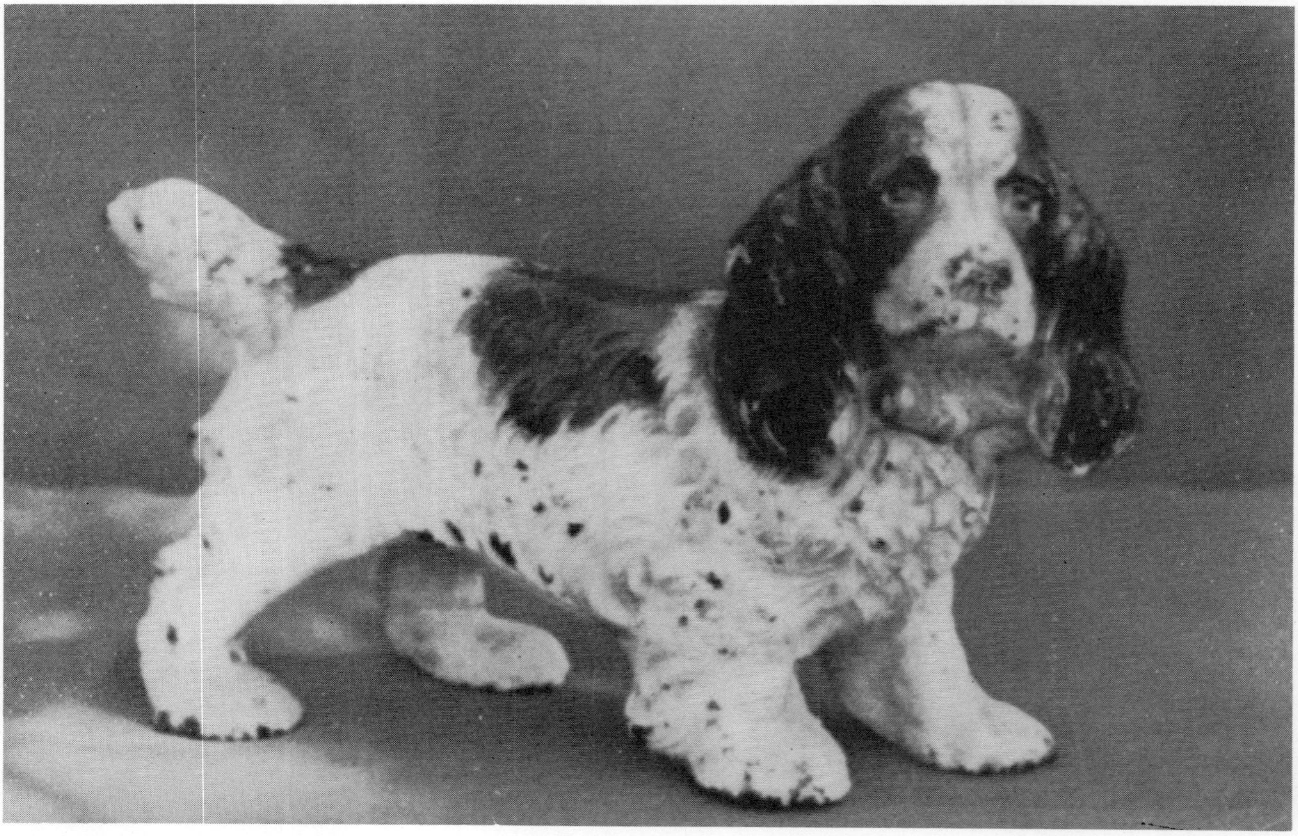

98. *Handsome cast-iron Cocker Spaniel.*

# Bibliography

### Ceramics

Barrett, Richard Carter. *How to Identify Bennington Pottery.* Brattleboro, Vermont: Stephen Green Press, 1964.

Quimby, M.G. *Ceramics in America-Winterthur Conference Report 1972.* Charlottesville, Virginia: University Press of Virginia, 1972.

Schwartz, Marvin. *Collector's Guide to Antique American Ceramics.* Garden City, New York: Doubleday and Co., 1969.

### Folk Art

Christensen, Erwin O. *Early American Wood Carving.* New York, N.Y.: Dover Publications, Inc., 1952.

Kauffman, Henry J. *Pennsylvania Dutch American Folk Art.* New York, N.Y.: American Studio Books, 1946.

Lichten, Francis. *Folk Art of Rural Pennsylvania.* New York, N.Y.: Charles Scribner's and Sons, 1946.

Lipman, Jean. *American Folk Art in Wood, Metal and Stone.* New York, N.Y.: Pantheon Press, 1948.

Museum of Modern Art. *American Folk Art, The Art of Common Man In America, 1750-1900.* New York, N.Y.: Arno Press, 1969.

Polley, Robert L., ed. *America's Folk Art. Treasures of American Folk Arts and Crafts in Distinguished Museums and Collections.* Waukesha, Wisconsin: Country Beautiful Corporation, 1971.

Robacher, Earl F. *Touch of the Dutchland.* Cranbury, New Jersey: A.S. Barnes and Co., Inc., 1965.

### Glass

Cloak, Evelyn Campbell. *Glass Paperweights of the Bergstrom Art Center.* New York, N.Y.: Bonanza Books, 1969.

Davis, Frank. *Continental Glass.* New York, N.Y.: Praeger Publishers.

Elville, E.M. *The Collector's Dictionary of Glass.* In *Country Life.* London: Spring Books, Drury House, 1967.

Lindsey, Bessie M. *American Historical Glass.* Rutland, Vermont: Charles E. Tuttle Co., 1966.

Wakefield, Hugh. *19th Century British Glass.* New York, N.Y.: Thomas Yoseloff Ltd., 1961.

Wills, Geoffrey. *England and Irish Glass.* New York, N.Y.: Doubleday and Co., Inc., 1968.

*Iron*

Hindle, Brooke. *Technology in Early America.* Chapel Hill, N.C.: University of North Carolina Press, 1968.
Kauffman, Henry J. *American Copper and Brass.* Camden, N.J.: Thomas Nelson, 1968.
_____. *Early American Ironware Cast and Wrought.* Rutland, Vermont: Charles E. Tuttle Co., 1966.
Lindsay, Seymour. *Iron and Brass Implements of the American Home.* Boston, Mass.: Herman Publishers, 1964.
Smith, Elmer L. *Early Iron Ware.* Lebannon, Pa.: Applied Arts Publishers, 1973.
Sylvia, J. Gerin. *Cast Metals Technology.* Reading, Mass.: Addison-Wesley Publishing Co., 1972.
Victoria and Albert Museum. *Old English Patterns of the Metal Trades.* In *Victoria and Albert Museum Catalog.* London: 1913.
Virginia Metalcrafters. *Gifts and Decorative Accessories.* Waynesboro, Va.: Virginia Metalcrafters, Inc., 1974.

*Victoriana*

*American Heritage,* eds. *The American Heritage History of Antiques from Civil War to World War I.* New York, N.Y.: American Heritage Publishing Co., Inc., 1969.
*Art-Journal. The Crystal Palace Exhibition Illustrated Catalogue, London 1851.* New York, N.Y.: Dover Publications, Inc., unabridged reproduction, special issue, 1970.
*Encyclopaedia Britannica.* London: William Benton Publisher, 1929.
D'Imperio, Dan. *The ABC's of Victorian Antiques.* New York, N.Y.: Dodd, Mead and Co., 1974.
Howe, Bea. *Antiques from the Victorian Home.* New York, N.Y.: Charles Scribner's Sons, 1973.
Hughes, Bernard. *Collecting Antiques.* New York, N.Y.: Macmillan Inc., 1961.
Hughes, Therle. *More Small Decorative Antiques.* New York, N.Y.: Macmillan Inc., 1963.
Israel, Fred L., ed. *Sears Roebuck Catalogue.* New York, N.Y.: Chelsea House Publishers, 1968.
Lichten, Francis. *Decorative Art of Victoria's Era.* New York, N.Y.: Charles Scribner's and Sons, 1950.
Mebane, John. "Door Porters, Good to Collect." In *The Antique Trader Weekly, Annual of Articles for 1972.* Dubuque, Iowa: Babka Publishing Co., 1950.
Michael, George. *The Basic Book of Antiques.* New York, N.Y.: Arco Publishing Co., Inc., 1974.
Norbury, James. *The World of Victoriana.* London: Hamlyn Publishing Group, Ltd., 1972.
Peter, Mary. *Collecting Victoriana.* New York, N.Y.: Frederick Praeger Publishers, Inc., 1968.
Phipps, Francis. *The Collector's Complete Dictionary of American Antiques.* Garden City, N.Y.: Doubleday and Co., Inc., 1974.
Read, Brian. *Regency Antiques.* London: William Clowes and Sons, Ltd., 1953.
Sellens, Alvin. *The Stanley Plane.* South Burlington, Vermont: The Early American Industries Association, 1975.

# *Index*

Ally Sloper, 27
Aluminum, 39
Art Deco, 36, 37, 38
Art Nouveau, 35, 36

Barnum, P.T., 54
Bear, cast iron, 50
Blowpipe, 18
Brass doorstops, 47
Bristol, 20
Britannia Foundry, 26
British Patent Office, 54
Brooklyn Museum, 18
Bronze, 39
Brunnerville Foundry, 28, 29
Buddha, 34, 35
"Buddy," 60

Casting, 45, 46, 47
Cat, wood, 21; china, 35; iron, 66
Centennial Exhibition of Philadelphia, 29, 31, 35
Chalk, 18
Chinaman, 35
Coaches, 55
Coalbrookdale Company, 24, 26
Coalport, 18
Collectible, 13
Colonial man, 55
Cope, 47
Copeland's model, 18
Copper, 44
Cornucopia, 24
Cornwall Furnace, 46
Crystal Palace Exhibition, 26

Derby, 18
Designs, German folk, 29, 31; reproduction, 43; stolen, 43
Diamond registration, 55
Doc Jim, 55, 64
Dog, boxer, 59; bulldog, 38; earthenware, 18; police, 38; scotty, 39; terrier, 38; tilted head, 55
Doorporter, English, 13; mechanism, 14; regency, 14, 15, 16, 25

Doorstop, American, 13; collectible, 13; forms, 47; weight, 63
Drag, 47
Dumps, 18
Dutch girl, 55

Earliest type, 14
Eastern Shore, 22
"End-of-day," 59
Eurasians, 45
Exhibition, Philadelphia Centennial, 29, 31, 35; Crystal Palace, 26

Fake, 61
Ferromania, 28
Flower baskets, Art Deco, 37; Brunnerville, 30; patent, 58; Pennsylvania German, 31; wood, 39, 95
Folk art, 13, 31, 32, 43
Forges, Mount Joy, 46; Valley, 46
Foundry, Britannia, 26; Brunnerville, 28, 29; St. Blazey, 25
Frog, bronze, 39, 41; pornographic, 24
Full-form figure, 47, 49
Full-mold, 47
Furnace, Cornwall, 46; Hopewell, 46

Glass, bubbles, 19; dump, 18; flint, 20; free-blown, 19; green, 18, 20
Gothic Knight, 26

Half-bell, 15
Handle, kinds, 15, 21
Handyside, Andy, 26
Harlow, Mabel, 56
Hopewell Furnace, 46
Hospitality, symbol, 15
Hubley, 46, 51

Iron manufacture, 43
Izon, John, 14

Jackson, Andrew, 27, 28
Japan, 34, 35
Japanned, 52
"Judy," 27

"Jumbo," 54

Kenrick, 16
Kinstler, Calvin Roy, 59
Knottingley, 20
Kutani, 35

Lind, Jenny, 31, 33
Lion's paw, 15
Locomotion, 26

Manual-training, 39
Marble, carving, 22; kinds, 22
Milliflori, 20
Monkey, 40
Mount Joy Forge, 46
Museum, Brooklyn, 18; Newark, 21; Tolson Memorial, 20

Nailsea, 20
Neo-Greek, 35

Orientalia, 34, 35
Origin, 14
Oxidation, 61

Paint, 31, 52
Patent, 36, 54; Office, 54
Pattern carver, 59
Peacock, 15, 35
Pickard, K. M., 38
Pig, 21
Pig iron, 46
Pineapple, 14, 15
Plinth, 15, 25
Popeye, 40
Poppy, 52
Punch, 24, 26, 27, 28, 62

Regency, 14, 15, 16; swan, 25

Reproductions, 60, 64; size, 63
Riser, 47
Rockingham, 18
Rubber, 39, 41
Rust, 61

St. Blazey, 25
St. Louis Malleable, 59
Sangus Ironworks, 45
*Sears and Roebuck Catalog of 1927*, 35; *1938-1939*, 38
Ship, rubber, 41
Smithsonian Institution, 22
Spanish dancer, 36, 38, 55
Sprue, 47
Staffordshire, 18
Stevenson's train, 26
Stoneware, cottages, 18
"Swedish Nightingale," 31

Tiffany, Louis, 35
"Ting-a-ling," 46
Tolson Memorial Museum, 20
Tools, 49
Tuteur, Charles, 56, 68

Valley Forge, 46
Victoriana, 24, 25, 29, 30, 34, 52
Virginia Metalcrafters, 52

Wakefield, 20
Washington, George, 31
Watkins, 22
Weaver, David S., 59
Wellington, 24
Whitehurst, Thomas, 14
Wilson, Woodrow, 38
Wood, kinds, 50
Worcester, 18